P9-DME-014

The Beginner's Guide

—

Pastels

*A complete step-by-step
guide to techniques and
materials*

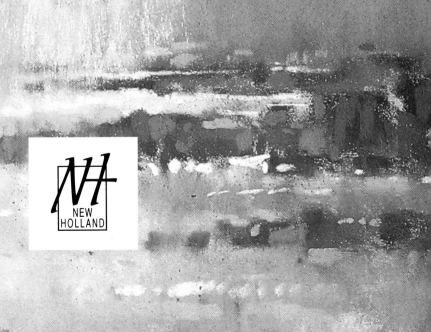

The Beginner's Guide

Pastels

A complete step-by-step guide to techniques and materials

ANGELA GAIR

NEW HOLLAND

First published in 1997
by New Holland Publishers (UK) Ltd
London • Cape Town • Sydney • Auckland

24 Nutford Place
London W1H 6DQ

80 McKenzie Street
Cape Town 8001
South Africa

Level 1, Unit 4 ·
14 Aquatic Drive
Frenchs Forest, NSW 2086
Australia

Unit 1A, 218 Lake Road
Northcote, Auckland
New Zealand

10 9 8 7 6 5

Copyright © 1997 New Holland Publishers (UK) Ltd

All rights reserved. No part of this publication may be reproduced,
stored in a retrieval system, or transmitted in any form or by any means,
electronic, mechanical, photocopying, recording or otherwise, without the prior written
permission of the publishers and copyright holders.

ISBN 1 85368 604 2 (pb)

Designed and edited by
Axis Design
311 Regents Park Road
London N3 1DP

Editor: Phyllis Richardson
Designer: Siân Keogh
Photographer: Chas Wilder

Reproduction by P & W Singapore
Printed and bound in Malaysia by Times Offset (m) sdn Bhd

ACKNOWLEDGEMENTS
Special thanks are due to Daler-Rowney, P.O Box 10, Bracknell, Berkshire, RG12 4ST,
Canson & Montgolfier Papers, Unit 26, Stephenson Road, St. Ives, Cambridgeshire and
Unison Colour, Thorneyburn, Tarset, Northumberland for providing the materials and
equipment featured in this book.

CONTENTS

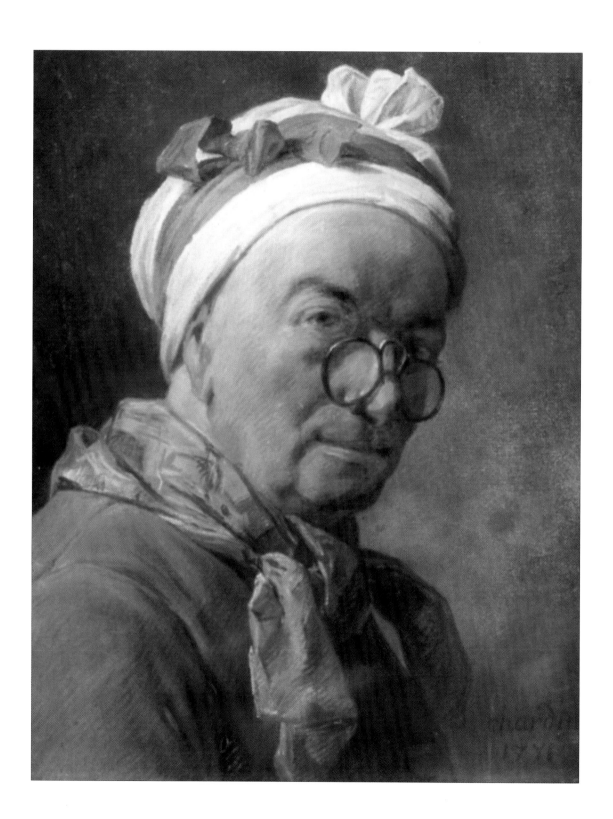

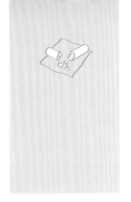

INTRODUCTION

Compared to other drawing and painting media, the history of pastel painting is comparatively short, and it was in eighteenth-century France that some of its earliest and finest exponents worked. The real pioneer of the medium was a Venetian woman, Rosalba Carriera (1674–1757), one of few female artists to have achieved fame in the visual arts before the nineteenth century. Her method, like that of all early pastelists, was to conceal the strokes of the chalk by smoothing and blending, thus giving an effect similar to an oil painting. She specialized in producing silk-smooth portraits of lords and ladies of the royal court and enjoyed a tremendous vogue when working in France during the regency of Louis XV.

It was Carriera who introduced Quentin de la Tour (1704–1788) to the pastel medium. Under her influence he became one of the most sought-after pastel portraitists of his day. The accomplished ease and rapidity with which he handled what he called his "coloured dust" helped him to capture a spontaneous expression of his sitters' personalities. "Unknown to them", he said, "I descend into the depths of my sitters and bring back the whole man."

Self-portrait with Glasses *Jean-Baptiste Simeon Chardin*

Chardin's works contrast with those of his contemporaries in that they are more solid and reflect the painter's search for realism. In this portrait fused and blended strokes are reserved mainly for the background; on the face, unblended open strokes of pastel describe the modulations from one plane to another and give life and animation to the drawing.

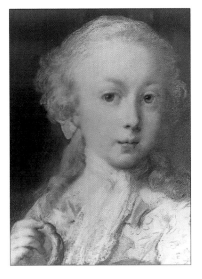

Portrait of a Young Girl *Rosalba Carriera*

Carriera, the pioneer of the pastel medium, used a very delicate and fused touch to produce extremely subtle grades of tone with barely a trace of individual strokes.

In France pastel painting became a craze and by 1780 there were hundreds of pastelists working in Paris, producing charming but somewhat vacuous portraits of aristocrats in all their finery, or sentimental studies of smiling, mischievous children, which have perhaps been responsible for giving the medium its undeserved reputation for superficiality.

The latter half of the eighteenth century, however, brought with it a renewed emphasis on realism, naturalness and honesty in painting, as evidenced in the pastel work of the great French master, Jean-Baptiste Simeon Chardin

(1699– 1779). Chardin only took up pastel when failing eyesight prevented him from continuing to paint in oils. Nevertheless, his contribution to the medium was important, for he broke with the tradition of his day and developed techniques that deliberately emphasized the marks of the pastel. He used superimposed layers of colour to build up a thick impasted texture, and he introduced methods of building form by juxtaposing strokes of pure colour without blending that were to be admired by Degas a century later.

Café-Concert at the Ambassadeurs *Edgar Degas*

Café life was very much a part of nineteenth-century culture, and formed the theme of many of Degas' works. He was particularly attracted to the effect of artificial illumination, such as the spotlights in this scene which produce a dramatic glare from beneath the figures on stage.

With the outbreak of the French Revolution in 1789, pastel fell out of favour for a time because it was associated too much with the frivolity and excesses of the *ancien régime*. It was the great Romanticist, Eugène Delacroix (1798–1863) who was responsible for its revival in the early nineteenth century. Both he and his compatriot Eugène Boudin (1824–1898) took their pastels into the countryside to make rapid sketches of sea, sky and land. For these *plein air* painters, pastel offered a medium well suited to recording the sudden excitement of visual sensations, the fresh colours of nature and the fleeting effects of light.

Given the speed, facility and brilliancy that pastels offer, it is surprising that the French Impressionists did not make more use of them in their efforts to capture the immediate and transient effects of light on the landscape. Even Edgar Degas (1834–1917) did not turn to pastels until his later years when, like Chardin before him, his fail-

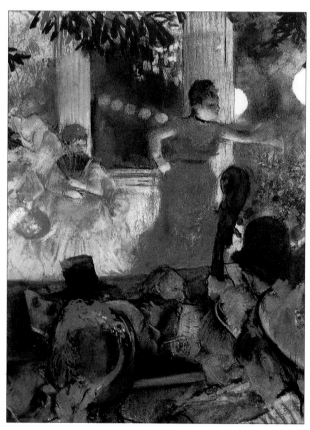

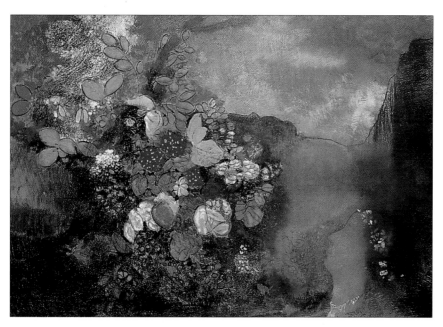

ing eyesight prevented him from working in oils. Unlike his contemporary Impressionists, Degas actively disliked outdoor painting, remarking that "The gendarmes should shoot down all those easels cluttering up the countryside." His reputation as the greatest pastelist of all time rests on his breathtakingly original compositions of indoor life, featuring dancers, café scenes and women washing or bathing.

Degas developed the pastel medium far beyond the traditional formulae of the eighteenth-century masters. He experimented with an incredible variety of strokes and combinations of strokes to render form, light and texture. At one time or another, he employed every pastel technique known and invented many new ones. For example, he frequently sprayed steam over his pastels or mixed them with fixative to form a paint-like paste that he could then work into with a stiff brush or his fingers.

Another innovation made by Degas, which opened up a whole new field for the twentieth-century artists, was his use of pastel and mixed media. He often built up densely textured layers of colours combining pastel, gouache, tempera and oil paints diluted with turpentine. He also frequently used pastels in combination with

Ophelia Among the Flowers *Odilon Redon*

Having worked in black and white media most of his life (mainly lithographs and charcoal drawings) Odilon Redon turned to pastels in the 1890s. Associated with the Symbolists, his central themes were flowers and mythological scenes, and he found the ethereal quality of pastel ideal for creating a dream-like atmosphere of mood and reverie. This picture, for example, is a meditation on the theme of youth and the ephemeral beauty of flowers.

monotypes; the print was used rather like an underdrawing, and the pastel colour was applied on top. He found this technique ideal for reproducing such visual effects as the gauzy, semi-transparent tutu of a ballerina.

Thanks to Degas, pastel in the twentieth century has been appreciated for its versatility and its powers of expression. The French artist Odilon Redon (1840–1916), for example, exploited the jewel-like colours of pastel in his symbolist paintings of flowers and mythological scenes. Modern pastel artists enjoy the "sculptural" qualities of pastel and its ability to be both a painting and a drawing medium, emphasizing its linearity and texture as well as its powdery insubstantiality.

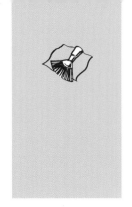

MATERIALS AND EQUIPMENT

Pastels are a unique and versatile medium, combining the speed and directness of drawing with the rich and varied range of colour associated with painting media.

Pastels are made from powder pigments that are mixed with a base such as chalk and bound together with gum to form a stiff paste which is then shaped into round or square sticks and allowed to harden.

Soft pastels are the most widely used of the various pastel types because they produce the wonderful velvety bloom that is so typical of the medium. They have a high proportion of pigment to binder, so the colours are rich and vibrant. Soft pastels are easy to blend and smudge to create rich, painterly effects.

Hard pastels contain more binder than the soft type, giving them a firmer texture suitable for adding linear details and crisp touches to soft pastel work. The colour range is limited compared to that of soft pastels, and they don't have the same luminosity and bloom.

Pastel pencils are thin, hard pastel sticks encased in wooden shafts. Clean and easy to control, they can be sharpened to a point to produce fine, firm lines.

Oil pastels contain an oil binder instead of gum and have a moist, waxy texture. They make thick, buttery strokes that are ideal for direct, spontaneous working. The colour can also be softened and spread to make "washes" by brushing with turpentine or white (mineral) spirit.

Inevitably you will build up a large stock of pastels of every hue, so it makes sense to store them separately according to colour in a box with several compartments.

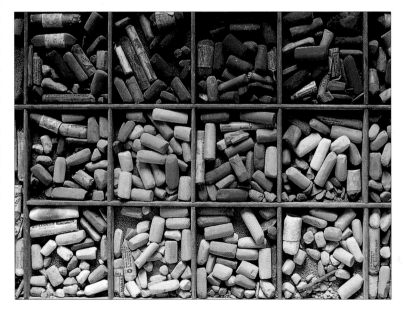

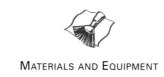

CHOOSING COLOURS

Pastel, not being a liquid medium in which a few colours can be mixed to create infinite combinations, requires a separate stick for every tone and hue. This explains why there are literally hundreds of different colours available, and why each individual colour comes in a range of tints and shades. The paler tints are achieved by adding progressively more white pigment to the full-strength colour, and the darker shades by adding black.

Each pastel stick is individually wrapped and identified by colour name and number; for example, in one brand each colour has no. 1 against its lightest tint, and no. 8 against its darkest tint. The system of numbering varies between brands.

No one can honestly prescribe a recommended palette of colours for pastel painting because the range of available colours (and their tints) is so vast, and the colours and colour names vary so widely from one brand to another. Also, much depends on your choice of subject. If you paint landscapes, you will obviously require a good selection of blues and greens; for portraiture, you will need more earth tones and reds. The best advice is to start off with a small boxed set of pre-selected colours and add to this with individual colours as you gain more experience. Soft pastels vary from one brand to the next regarding the degree of softness and the range of colours; one brand, for example, may feature more bright hues while another tends towards the subtler colours, and there is no reason why you should not "mix and match" brands.

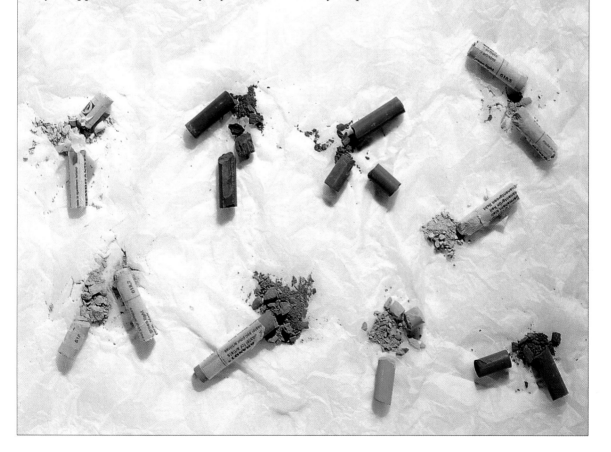

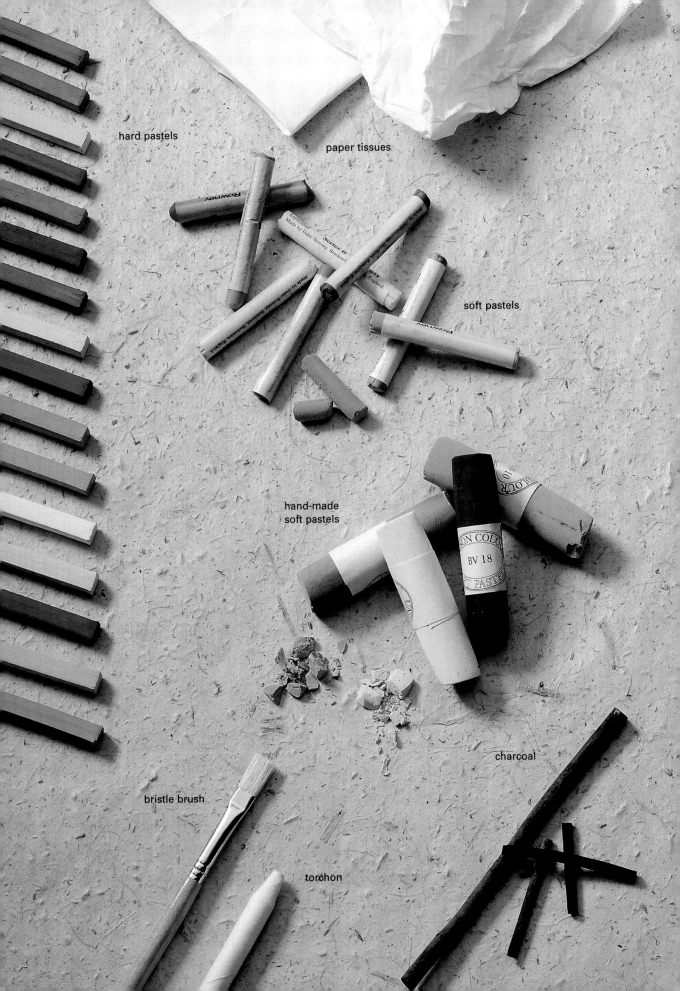

hard pastels

paper tissues

soft pastels

hand-made
soft pastels

charcoal

bristle brush

torchon

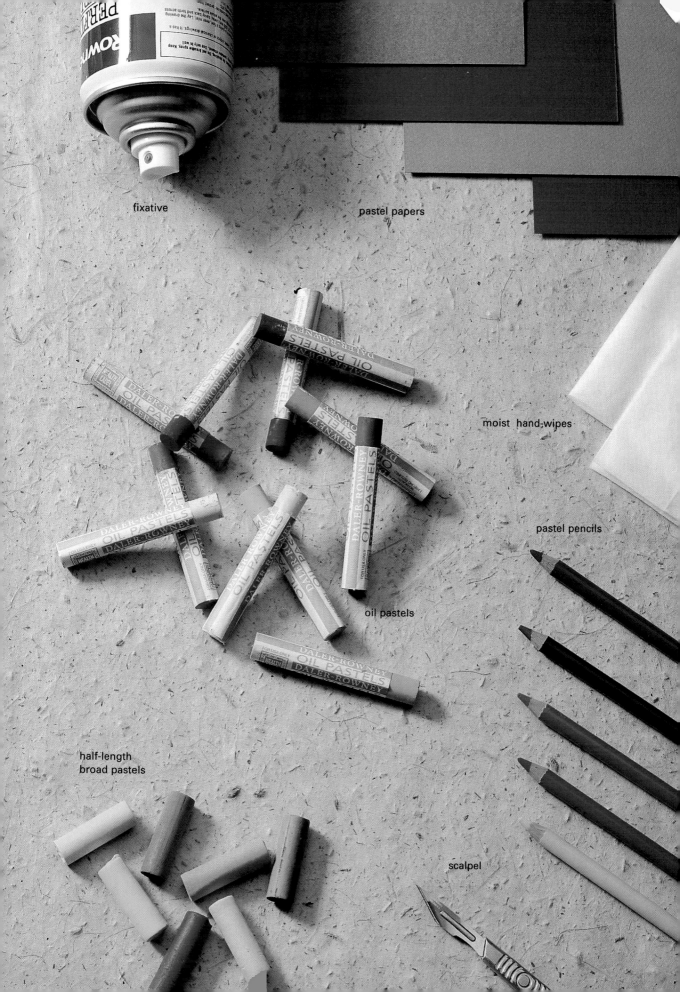

fixative

pastel papers

moist hand-wipes

pastel pencils

oil pastels

half-length
broad pastels

scalpel

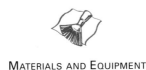
SURFACES

Pastel papers are available in a wide range of colours and are usually more textured on one side than the other, allowing you to choose the surface best suited to your technique. The two best-known papers sold for pastel work are Ingres (which has a laid pattern of small, regular lines) and Mi-Teintes (which has a fine "wire mesh" pattern).

Sansfix The unique tooth of this paper, similar to very fine glasspaper, is made from a thin layer of fine cork particles. It holds the pastel particles so well that fixing the finished painting is not necessary.

Watercolour paper is tough and hard-wearing, and excellent for pastel painting so long as it is a rough-textured one; smooth papers don't have enough tooth to grip and hold the layers of pigment. Tinted watercolour papers are now available. You can also tint white paper with watercolour or with other water-based paints. Alternatively, apply a dry wash with pastel powder (see page 16).

Charcoal paper is inexpensive, but it is rather thin and fragile and has a rather mechanical surface texture. Use it for rough sketches and practice work.

Velour paper has a soft surface like velvet and produces a rich, matt finish more like a painting than a drawing.

Fine glasspaper has a granular surface and provides a very good buff middle tone which is suitable for most subjects. The texture grips the particles of colour well.

Canvas and cotton fabrics, mainly sold for oil painting, can be stretched on a wooden stretcher or glued to board and used for pastel painting. The pronounced texture of canvas allows for a rich build-up of colour layers.

In choosing a surface for pastel painting there are three important factors to bear in mind: texture, colour and tone.

TEXTURE

Pastel requires a support with plenty of "tooth" to bite the particles of pigment and hold them in place. It is important that the pastel does not fill the tooth of the paper immediately; once the grain is lost, the pastel sticks begin to slide on the surface, making it difficult to deposit more colour.

COLOUR

Because areas of the background are often left uncovered in pastel work, the colour of the paper can make an important contribution to the finished image. Thus when selecting a paper you should bear in mind the effect you wish to achieve. First, decide whether you want the paper's colour to harmonize with the subject or complement it. Then decide whether the colour should be warm or cool. For example, you might choose a paper with a warm earth colour to accentuate the cool greens of a landscape; or you

a range of canson pastel papers

Ingres pastel paper

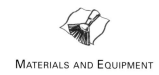

might choose a cool grey paper to provide a ready-made mid-tone for a stormy sky.

TONE

"Tone" refers to the relative lightness or darkness of the paper. Mid-toned papers are generally the most sympathetic for pastel paintings as they provide a harmonious backdrop to most colours and make it easy to judge the lights and darks in the image accurately. If the paper is too light in colour the darks can jump out at you, and vice versa.

ACCESSORIES

Fixative A pastel painting is a fragile thing that can be easily smudged unless it is handled with proper care. Protect finished pictures with fixative – a thin, colourless varnish that fixes the pastel particles to the surface and forms a thin, clear, protective coating. Fixative is most commonly available in aerosol spray cans, which are convenient to use and cover a large area quickly. However, the spray does give off unpleasant fumes that take some time to disperse. Alternatively, you can purchase mouth diffusers, which have a plastic mouthpiece through which a fine mist of fixative is blown.

Torchons (paper stumps) are tightly rolled paper "pencils" that are used for blending and spreading applied pastel colours. You can use your fingertip just as easily, but torchons are rigid and pointed at the tip, so are quite useful for blending small areas and intricate details.

A craft knife, scalpel or one-sided safety razor blade is good for sharpening pastel sticks and pastel pencils to a point so that they can be used for drawing fine details and for gently scraping away any unwanted layers of pastel. You can also use the craft knife or razor to scratch highlights, texture and details into an oil-pastel drawing.

A stiff brush (a worn-out bristle oil-painting brush is ideal) is handy for making corrections by removing surface pastel pigment.

Charcoal is ideal for the initial drawing stage as it dusts off easily, leaving a "ghost" image that can be worked over later with pastels.

Tissues are useful for blending colours and for "knocking back" charcoal underdrawings. Moist hand-wipes are also good to have around for keeping your fingers clean as you work.

Pastel can be used on a wide range of papers and boards. Always choose a surface that is durable and lightfast.

Not-surface watercolour paper

Mi-Teintes pastel paper

primed canvas

glasspaper

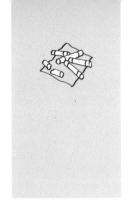

BASIC TECHNIQUES

TINTING THE SURFACE

There is an extensive range of coloured papers and boards for pastel painting, but you can also work on a textured white surface, such as watercolour paper, and tint it with a thin wash of watercolour, gouache or acrylic paint. (Lightweight papers will need to be stretched first, to prevent buckling when the wet colour is applied.) In this way you can achieve the precise colour value you require, and even produce tonal or colour variations rather than a flat, uniform area of colour. You can also rub damp tea leaves or a tea bag over the paper to obtain a pleasing warm tint.

Canvas and muslin-covered board can also be tinted with a thin wash of water-based paint such as gouache or acrylic.

Alternatively, you can tint the surface subtly with a "dry wash" of pastel powder. Reduce the pastel stick to a fine powder by scraping the edge with a sharp blade (or save the broken ends of pastel sticks and crush them to a powder with a palette knife). Use a large soft brush or a cotton ball to pick up the powder and spread it over the paper. Work it well into the grain, laying down a thin tint of colour.

MAKING MARKS

Pastel is a wonderfully expressive medium to draw with, so responsive it is almost like an extension of the artist's hand. Discover the expressive potential of the medium by making random marks on sheets of paper. Try using both hard and soft pastels, on rough and smooth-textured papers. A soft pastel on smooth paper glides effortlessly, leaving behind a satiny trail of vibrant colour; the same pastel used on rough paper gives a splattered, irregular line as the tooth of the paper breaks up the colour.

Dry Wash

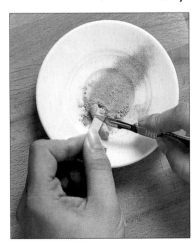

1

Use a craft-knife blade to scrape the edge of the pastel stick and create a fine powder. Hold the pastel over a dish to catch the powder as it falls.

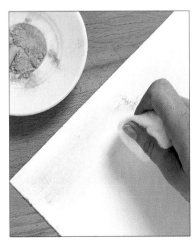

2

Dab a cotton ball into the powder and rub it across the surface. Further tones or colours can be added and blended on the paper surface.

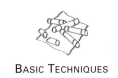
LINEAR STROKES

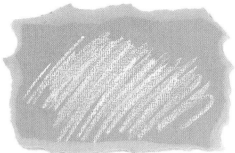

Loose hatching

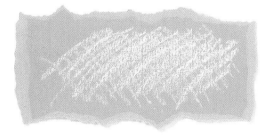

Crosshatching

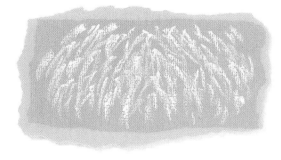

Stabbing marks

SIDE STROKES

Blended side strokes

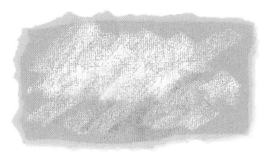

Scumbled side strokes

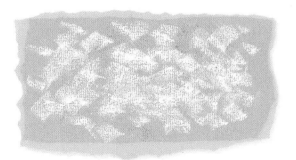

Stabbing marks

LINEAR STROKES

Use the point of the pastel, or snap the stick in two and use the sharp corners, to create linear marks. By varying the pressure on the stick and twisting and turning it you can produce lines that swell and taper.

You can also use line work to create subtle blends of tones and colours with techniques such as feathering, hatching and crosshatching.

SIDE STROKES

Snap off a short length of pastel and use it on its side to make broad bands of grainy colour. The depth of tone or colour depends on the pressure you apply and the texture of the paper. Heavy pressure forces more pastel into the tooth of the paper to create a dense, velvety quality; light pressure produces a delicate veil of colour through which the texture and colour of the paper, or a previous layer of pastel, is visible – a technique called scumbling.

Use ground rice to clean your pastels. The small plastic tray shown here also comes in handy as a lightweight, easy-to-hold "palette" in which to keep the particular colours you need for a painting.

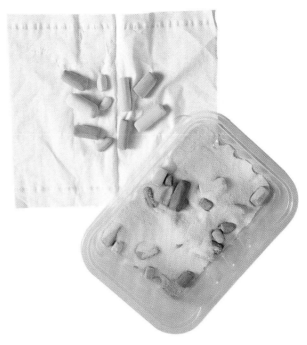

CLEANING PASTELS

Pastels get dirty through handling – after a while they all look the same dusty grey colour. To clean your pastels, pop them in a container filled with ground rice and shake gently. The gritty texture of the rice rubs away the surface dirt and in no time at all your pastels emerge sparkling once more. Sieve to remove the dirtied rice.

ERASING PASTEL

While the pastel is still thinly applied and fairly loose on the surface, the best way to erase mistakes is to use a stiff-bristled paintbrush to flick away the powdery colour.

Conventional rubber erasers tend to flatten the texture of the paper and smear the pastel into the grain instead of lifting it off.

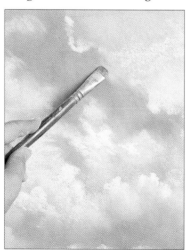

A kneaded or putty eraser can be useful for lightening a small area to obtain a highlight. Press the eraser on the spot and gently lift the loose colour off with a dabbing motion. A small piece of bread gently rolled between the fingers can also be used.

In general it is best to avoid erasing in the later stages of a painting, as any method you use interferes with the natural texture of the pastel strokes and can spoil the paper surface. The best course, at a late stage, is to spray the area with fixative and rework it.

FIXING PASTELS

Pastel paintings can be protected from smudging by spraying with fixative. When you spray be careful not to saturate the

Use a bristle paintbrush to remove excess pastel pigment.

drawing as this darkens the colours and merges the pigment particles. The idea is to produce a fine mist that floats down lightly over the pastel. It is worth practising on pieces of scrap paper until you discover how to produce a fine mist without getting any drips on the paper.

First, tap the board to dislodge all the loose particles of pigment. Standing at least 30cm (12in) from the easel, begin spraying just beyond the top left side of the picture. Work swiftly down the picture, spraying with a steady back-and-forth motion, always going beyond the edges of the picture before stopping. Keep your arm moving so that the spray doesn't build up in one area and create a dark patch or drip down the paper.

Always work in a room with adequate ventilation to avoid excessive inhalation of the spray.

ALTERNATIVE METHODS

Some artists avoid fixing unless it is absolutely necessary, on the grounds that it diminishes the brilliance of the colours and spoils the velvety surface bloom of the pastel. However, there are ways to get round the problem and still give your work a degree of protection from smudging. Try spraying lightly at intervals while working to seal the surface so that colours can be overlaid without muddying. Leave the last layer free so that the work retains its freshness.

Since the spray affects the lighter colours most, another alternative is to lightly spray the finished work and then pick out the light tones again.

Unless you are using a heavy paper or board, you can spray a light mist over the back of the paper. The fixative will soak through and hold the pigment without damaging the surface.

An alternative to spraying with fixative is to lay a sheet of smooth paper over the painting, then cover it with a board and apply pressure. This pressure fixes the pastel particles more firmly into the grain of the paper without affecting its surface.

Finally, there is a theory that pastel fixes itself in the course of time due to the presence of moisture in the air. Before framing a finished pastel, try leaving it on a shelf with air circulating freely around it for three or four weeks to allow the humidity of the room to help set the colour.

Squaring Up

You may wish to base a pastel painting on a photographic image or a sketch; but it is often difficult to maintain the accuracy of the drawing when enlarging or reducing a reference source to the size of your paper or board. A simple method of transferring an image in a different scale is by squaring up (sometimes called scaling up).

Using a pencil and ruler, draw a grid of equal-sized squares over the sketch or photograph. The more complex the image, the more squares you should draw. If you wish to avoid marking the original, make a photocopy of it and draw the grid onto this. Alternatively, draw the grid onto a sheet of clear acetate placed over the original, using a felt-tip pen.

Then construct an enlarged version of the grid on your support, using light charcoal lines. This grid must have the same number of squares as the smaller one. The size of the squares will depend on the degree of enlargement required: for example, if you are doubling the size of your reference material, make the squares twice the size of the squares on the original reference drawing or photograph.

When the grid is complete, transfer the image that appears in each square of the original to its equivalent square on the support. The larger squares on the working sheet serve to enlarge the original image. You are, in effect, breaking down a large-scale problem into smaller, more manageable, areas.

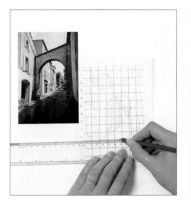

1 Make a sketch from the reference photograph and draw a grid of squares over it.

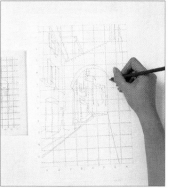

2 Draw a grid of larger squares onto the support and transfer the detail from the sketch, square by square.

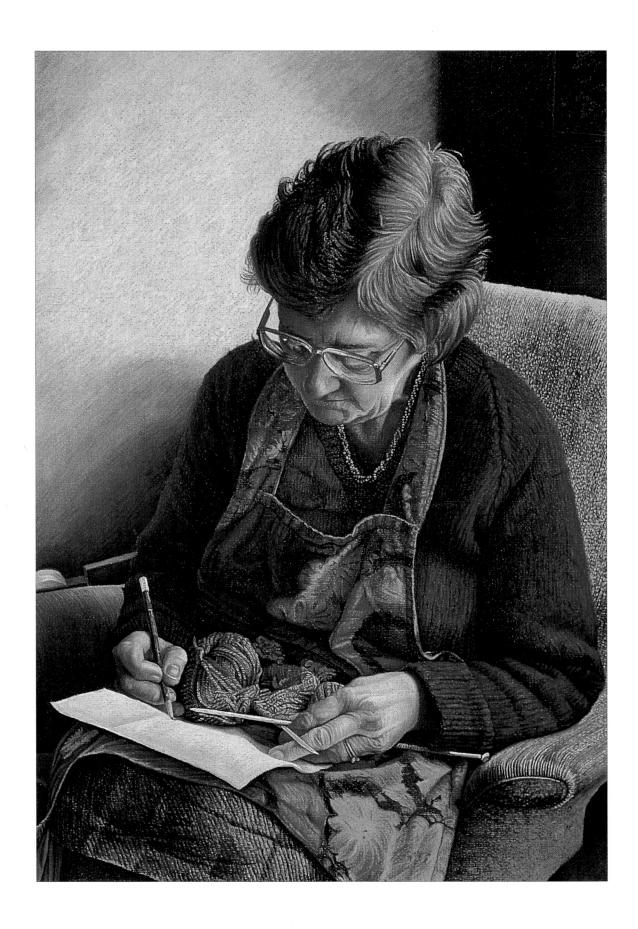

GALLERY

Pastels are a unique and versatile medium, combining the speed and directness of drawing with the rich and varied range of colour associated with painting media. Working with the pastel tip enables the artist to exploit the calligraphic qualities of line and contour, while using the long side of the pastel resembles painting with a broad brush to create soft fields of luminous colour.

There are many ways of applying pastel, and the "painting" and "drawing" techniques can be used alongside each other to produce a breathtaking range of effects. The small gallery of images that follows has been selected to demonstrate the expressive potential of pastel work, and represents a wide variety of styles, subjects and techniques.

Mother
Paul Bartlett
64 x 43cm (25 x 17in)

One of the most striking features of this portrait is the pin-sharp detail, not normally associated with the powdery, insubstantial nature of pastels. Bartlett uses countless tiny strokes to build up a variety of textures, giving the picture a sense of heightened reality.

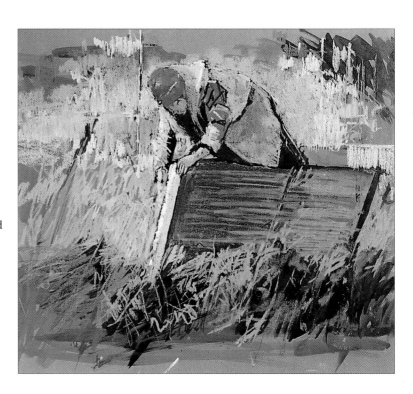

Mending the Fence
Barry Freeman
51 x 67cm (20 x 26in)

This is a study for a painting in oils. The artist washed in the broad areas with gouache paint, then used pastel to provide additional detail and textural contrast. Gouache and pastel are ideal partners, both being opaque media with brilliant colour qualities. The sketch is worked very freely, with large areas of the buff paper left uncovered to provide a unifying middle tone.

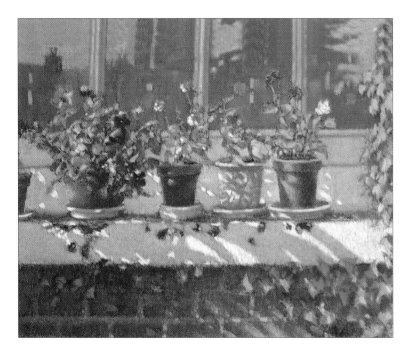

Windowsill, Summer
Derek Daniells
33 x 46cm (13 x 18in)

We tend to think of still life as a group of objects arranged against a background, but "found" groups, such as this row of potted plants on a windowsill, have a refreshingly uncontrived quality. Daniells combined blended and linear marks here to suggest the softly dappled quality of the light.

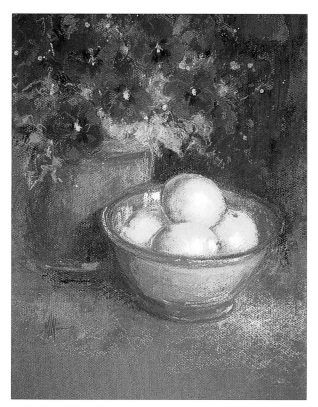

Bowl of Lemons
Maureen Jordan
37 x 29cm (14½ x 11½in)

The chiaroscuro effect of light in this still life was achieved with the aid of acrylic paints. Thin washes were washed onto the background to establish the deepest darks, which are difficult to attain with pastel colours. The image was then built up using hard pastels initially and then soft pastels in the final stages.

Farmhouse, Provence
Alan Oliver
28 x 38cm (11 x 15in)

Here the artist freely combines areas of broken colour with a variety of linear marks to build a complex, rich impression of colour and texture. The grain of the paper breaks up the pastel strokes, enhancing the lively quality of the image.

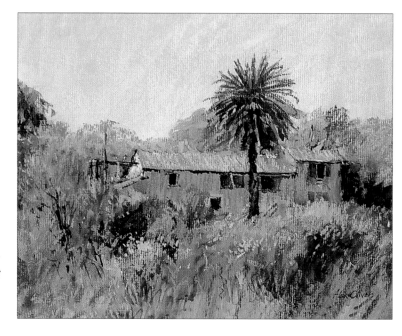

Figs, Plums and Grapes
John Ivor Stewart
36 x 51cm (14 x 20in)

By tightly cropping his subject the
artist gives it maximum impact.
In effect, we enjoy the picture on
two levels: first as a finely
observed study of natural forms
and textures, and second as a
rhythmic pattern of harmonious
shapes and colours.

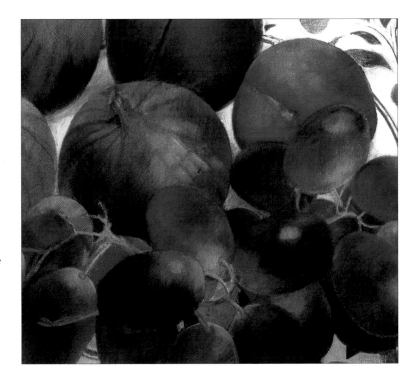

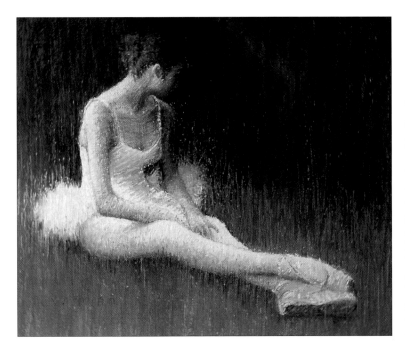

Waiting in the Wings
Charmian Edgerton
30 x 38cm (12 x 15in)

This study was worked on a
textured ground, which breaks up
the strokes of soft, friable pastel
and creates a striated, flickering
effect that accentuates the play of
light on the figure. The dark
background contains no black but
consists of an optical mix of
browns, greens and indigos;
similarly, the dancer's white tutu,
tights and pumps comprise strokes
of yellow, pink, blue and green.

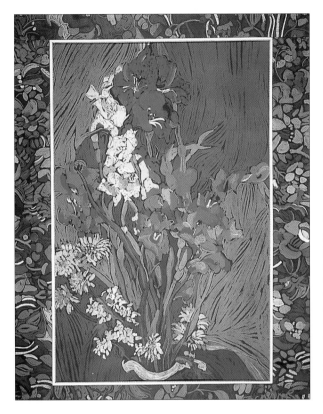

Gladioli
Frances Treanor
112 x 81cm (44 x 32in)

This flower portrait contains a riot of colour, but the diversity is tempered by a strong sense of design. The exuberant impact of the image is enhanced by the tension between the vivid pinks of the flowers and the equally vivid blue of the background, which sets up a push-pull vibration. The decorative border is a feature of Treanor's paintings, echoing and containing the colours in the main image.

After the Storm, Walberswick
Barry Freeman
38 x 49cm (15 x 19in)

This painting captures a moment in a shifting pattern of light which so characterizes the climate of northern Europe. A heavy rainstorm has just passed and sunlight breaks through the banks of cloud. Freeman has caught the glittering quality of the light using a high-key palette of pinks, blues and mauves. Lively, scumbled strokes throughout denote a sense of vibrancy while unifying the elements of sky and landscape.

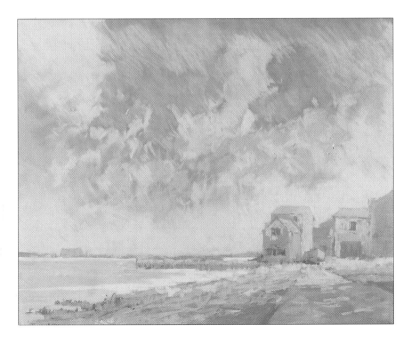

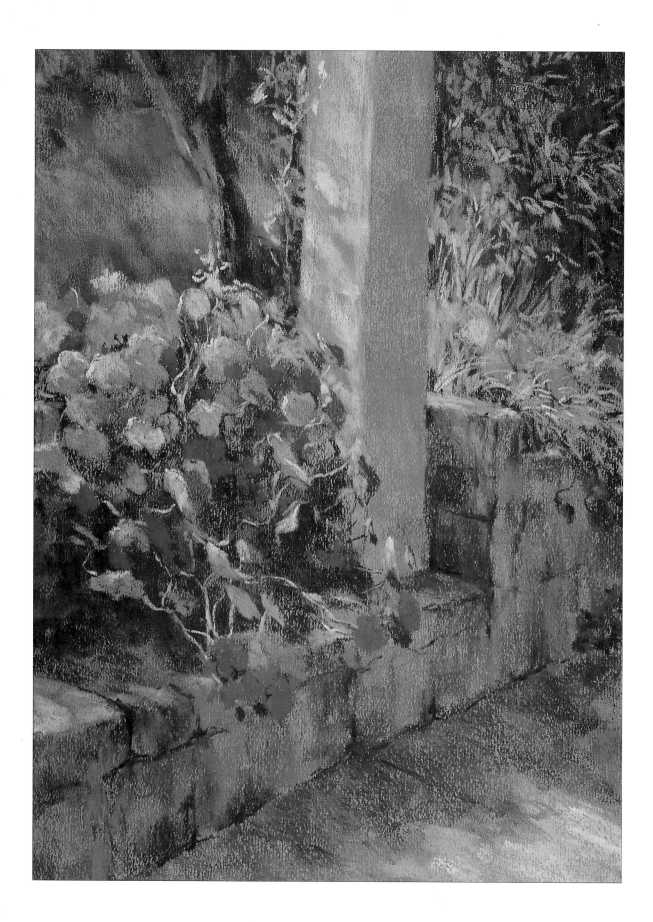

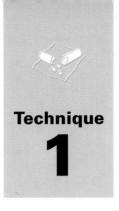

OVERLAYING COLOUR

This painting reflects the artist's delight in recreating the effects of light on the landscape. Bright sunlight filters down through the trees, casting dappled patterns on the cool, shadowy patio and brightly illuminating a flower here, a leaf there. A rich and exciting surface is achieved through the combined techniques of blocking in broad colour areas with the side of the pastel and drawing into shapes with the pastel tip.

Although the composition itself is quite simple, there is a lot of texture and detail in the flowers and foliage – subjects that can all too easily become overworked and muddy. In order to make sense of the complex mass of flowers, grasses and foliage, the artist began by blocking in the composition with thin layers of colour applied with the side of the pastel. From this initial "underpainting" she was able gradually to work up detail and intensify colour, creating the impression of massed foliage without clogging the paper surface.

Jackie Simmonds
Sunlit Patio
51 x 41cm (20 x 16in)

BUILDING UP THE PAINTING

Whereas an aqueous medium such as watercolour sinks into the body of the paper, dry, powdery pastel pigment more or less sits on the surface. If you apply too many heavy layers of colour, especially in the early stages, the tooth of the paper quickly becomes clogged and the pigment eventually builds up to a solid, slippery surface that resists further applications of colour.

To avoid this, you need to pace yourself in the early stages – it is a mistake to try to get to the finished picture too soon. A successful method of building up a pastel painting is to start by rapidly laying in the broad shapes and colour masses of the composition with thin colour before starting to develop the detail. Snap off a short length of pastel and block in the main colour areas, using side strokes to apply broad patches of grainy colour. These initial layers should be lightweight and open-textured; work lightly and loosely, stroking the colour on in thin veils and leaving plenty of paper showing between the strokes.

Overlaying thin, loose strokes of pigment in this way allows you to build up tones and colours gradually, without overworking the surface, so that when you come to accentuate the detail with linear marks and thicker colour towards the end of the picture, the colours will remain fresh and the strokes distinct.

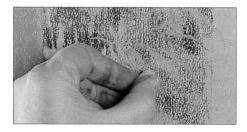

It is important to keep the surface of the picture light and open in the early stages, to avoid clogging the paper with pigment and making the surface unworkable.

SUNLIT PATIO

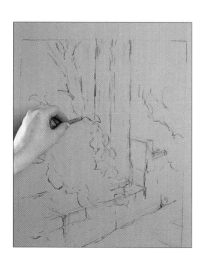

1
Sketch in the main outlines of the composition using charcoal. Draw with a light touch, keeping the lines loose and sketchy so that you can easily brush them off if you need to make alterations.

Materials and Equipment

• SHEET OF MEDIUM-TONED GREY FABRIANO PASTEL PAPER • THICK PASTEL STICKS: WARM RED, BRILLIANT RED, COOL RED, BRIGHT, GREENISH YELLOW, DARK GREEN, A RANGE OF LIGHT, WARM GREENS, DARK BLUE, DARK, MEDIUM- AND LIGHT-TONED UMBERS AND OCHRES, LIGHT TINT OF WARM OCHRE, BLUE-GREY, LIGHT TONE OF TURQUOISE GREEN • STICK OF CHARCOAL • SPRAY FIXATIVE

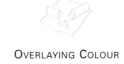

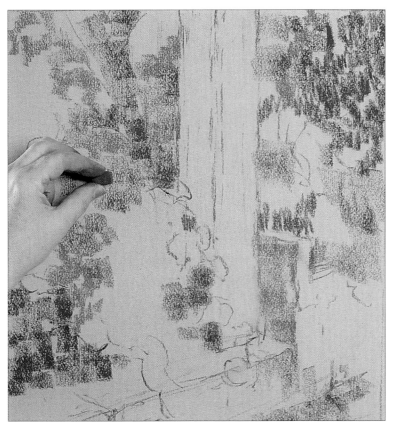

2

Rough in the main areas of light and dark tone, using a range of dark blues, greens and earth colours to establish the dark colour values of the background tree and foliage and the shadows in the foreground. Snap off short lengths of pastel and lightly stroke the colour on with the side of the stick, using short, broken marks that allow the colour of the paper to show through.

3

Using the same technique, block in the stone column and wall in the foreground using a light tint of warm ochre. Indicate the shadows on the column with a light tint of blue-grey, gently breaking it over the underlying colour with light, feathery strokes, allowing the warm ochre to show through and suggest the "glowing" effect of reflected light bouncing back into the shadows.

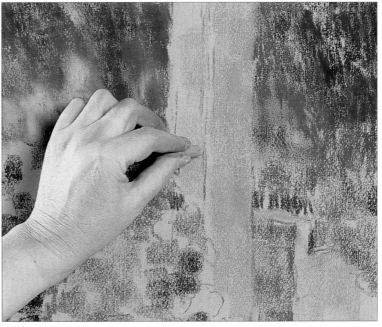

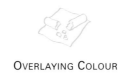

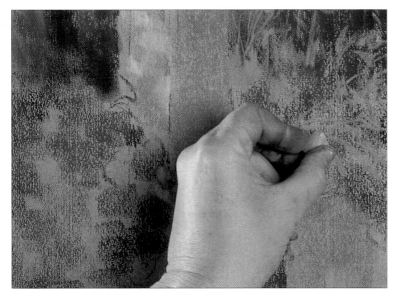

4

Apply broken strokes of very light ochre to indicate patches of dappled sunshine on the column. Now that the lights, darks and mid-tones are established, you can begin to build up the image with more colour and detail. Suggest the sunlit leaves and grasses in the background using a light, warm green. This time use the chisel edge of the stick to make linear strokes of varying lengths, and in various directions, to suggest leaves, tendrils and stalks.

5

Use the same green to paint the nasturtium leaves tumbling over the wall, using a short length of pastel on its side to make broad blocks of colour suggesting the fat, rounded forms of the leaves.

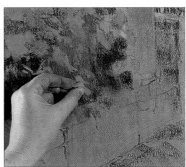

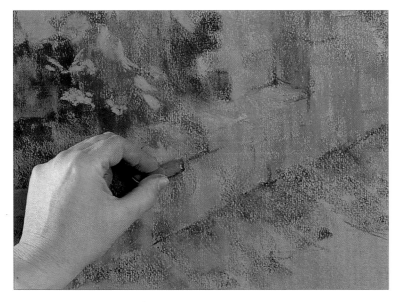

6

Before developing the nasturtiums any further, build up colour and texture on the wall using a mid-toned yellow ochre and a darker tone of burnt umber. Lay the colours over each other with broad side strokes in a vertical direction to indicate blocks of stone. Lay some of this colour over the cast shadow below the wall, too. Indicate a few fissures in the rock using the chisel edge of a dark blue pastel. Don't overdo it – just one or two broken, linear marks is all you need to suggest the crumbling texture of the wall.

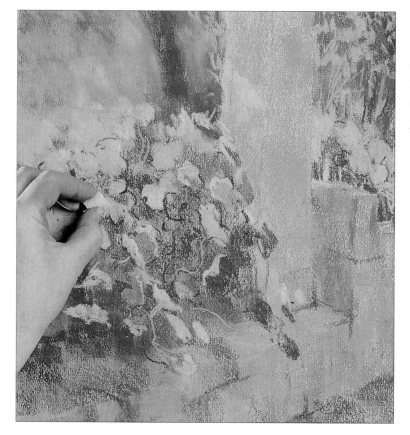

7

Using the same dark blue, pick out and define the edges of some of the nasturtium leaves, then block in the lightest tones on the sunlit leaves using a light tint of turquoise-green. Lightly spray-fix the picture so that you can add further layers of colour.

8

For the nasturtium flowers you will need two reds: a bright, warm one for the nearer blooms, and a slightly cooler, bluer one for those further back. Draw the flowers with scribbled strokes, suggesting their shapes rather than defining them too clearly and losing the spontaneity of the image. Vary the shape and size of the flowers, making them larger in the foreground and gradually getting smaller farther back.

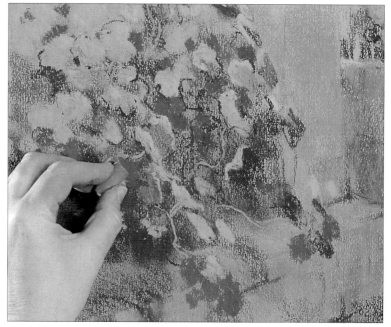

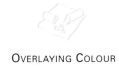

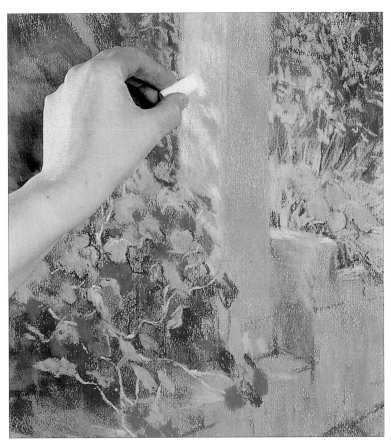

9

Use a warm, yellowish green to draw the sunlit tendrils and stalks of the nasturtiums with light, broken lines. Then add more dappled highlights on the column and the top of the wall using a very light tint of ochre. Apply a little more pressure with the pastel stick now, to give the highlights more definition. Stroke some of the same colour onto the road in the immediate foreground.

10

Deepen the shadows on the wall and road with side strokes of bluish grey applied with a light touch so that the underlying colours glow through. Then add the brightest highlights on the flowers, using a brilliant poppy red. Don't be tempted to overdo these highlights, though – brilliant spots of colour are more effective when used sparingly.

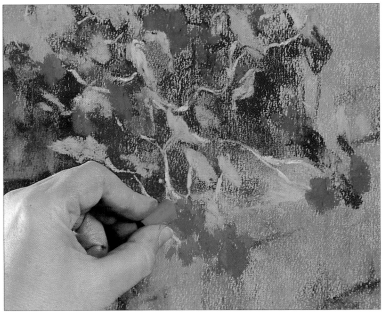

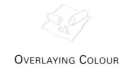

11

Develop the background, applying strokes of warm ochre on the sunlit side of the tree and suggesting the shifting patterns of light and shadow on the grass using a warm yellow green and a cool turquoise green. Gently blend the colours with the tip of your finger; these broad masses, in contrast with the sharper detail in the foreground, help to increase the illusion of space and depth in the picture.

Use a light greenish yellow to draw the creeper twining up the column and to accent the light-struck leaves and tendrils, mainly along the top edge of the flowers but also where the sun catches here and there near the bottom of the wall.

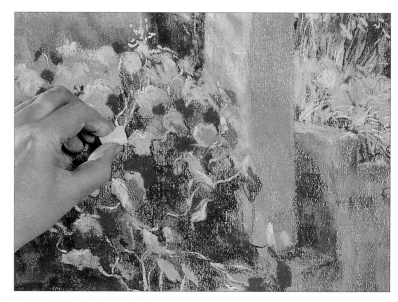

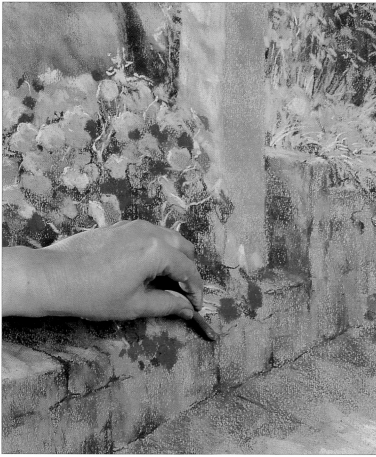

12

Finally, suggest the crumbling texture of the wall using a thin charcoal stick to lightly draw in a few cracks and fissures.

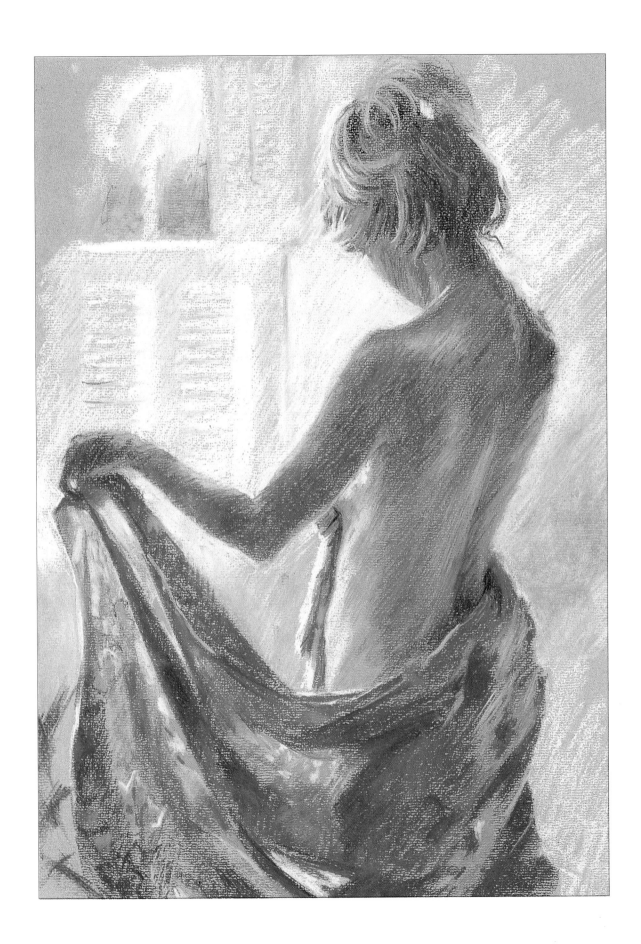

Technique
2

FEATHERING

In painting something as delicate as the skin of a young woman, it is tempting for the inexperienced pastelist to blend and rub the colours in trying to create the soft gradations of the skin tones. Yet the result is often more likely to be somewhat "sugary", superficial and lifeless.

In this painting the artist has done the exact opposite, relying on the linear marks made by the pastels to build up the structure of the figure. She has mixed her colours by laying light, feathery strokes of opposing colours, one on top of the other, to create new and brilliant hues. This juxtaposition, which calls upon the viewer's eye to mix and blend colours, produces a shimmering and vibrant interpretation of the skin tones and imbues the work with energy and life. The soft, friable pastel pigment catches on the raised tooth of the paper, creating a striated, flickering effect between the layers of warm and cool colour that accentuates the play of light on the figure.

Hazel Soan
Woman with Sarong
56 x 41cm (22 x 16in)

FEATHERING TECHNIQUE

The term "feathering" describes a linear technique used for creating exciting colour mixes in pastel. Colours are laid next to and over each other using the tip of the pastel to make quick, light, linear strokes, keeping the direction of the strokes consistent.

Similar to other broken-colour techniques, such as scumbling and pointillism, feathering is a way to integrate a range of hues and to blend them optically, in the eye of the viewer, rather than physically on the support. Particularly vibrant areas of colour can be achieved by feathering complementary colours, such as red and green, or yellow and violet, over one another. In addition, the feathered strokes create an active surface effect that adds a further dimension to the finished picture. The many touches of colour add a luminous quality to the surface, making it shimmer and dance with light.

Feathering is also a useful way to revive a particular area of colour that has become lifeless through excessive blending or rubbing in. Simply make light, feathery strokes of a contrasting colour over the blended area. Be careful to let the underlying colour show through and become enlivened, but not covered, by the overlaid strokes. Feathered strokes can also be used to tie together and unify shapes and colours and to soften hard edges.

Similarly, feathering provides a means of subtly altering or enriching colours without having to resort to erasing or scraping. For example, a red that looks too "hot" can be easily cooled down by feathering over it with strokes of its complementary colour, green, and vice versa. The secret is not to press too hard; use a light, feathery touch that causes the colour to float on top of the existing one.

WOMAN WITH SARONG

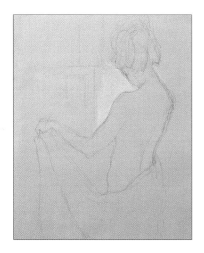

1 Using fine willow charcoal or a graphite stick, lightly sketch the figure and suggest the background. Avoid making solid, continuous outlines but let your pencil move lightly over the paper, feeling out the forms.

Materials and Equipment
- SHEET OF GREY CANSON PASTEL PAPER • SOFT PASTELS: WARM RED, WARM RED BROWN, PURPLE-RED, PALE ORANGE, PALE YELLOW, DARK BROWN, DARK COLD GREEN, PALE TURQUOISE GREEN, LIGHT PURPLE, DARK PURPLE, PALE BLUE AND WHITE
- CHARCOAL OR GRAPHITE STICK

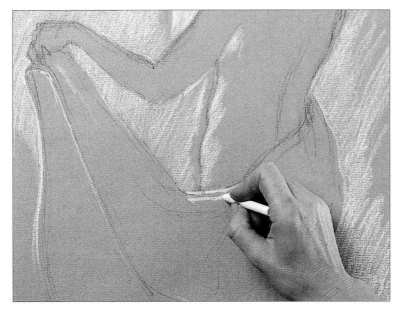

2

Block in the light tones behind the figure with loosely hatched diagonal strokes, using the tip of a white charcoal stick. Suggest the reflected light on the front of the figure and position the main folds in the cotton sarong she is holding.

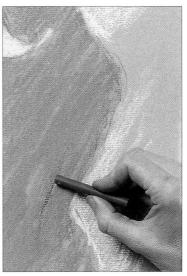

3

Use a warm, reddish brown to block in the figure with loosely spaced hatching, allowing the colour of the paper to show through. Apply light pressure so as not to clog the grain of the paper. Use the same colour to define the darkest shadows on the fabric, where it wraps around the model's body. Lightly draw the indent of the spine with a darker brown.

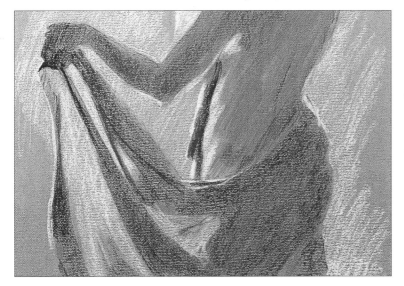

4

Use strokes of white and a cool, purplish red to build up the highlights, folds and creases in the wrap, lightly feathering the colour over the brown underlayer to deepen the tone of the darker shadows. Add touches of this cool red on the back of the model's head, across her shoulders and on her arm, which are in shadow. Use a warmer red on the hand, and at the front edge of the wrap, which reflect warm light from the window.

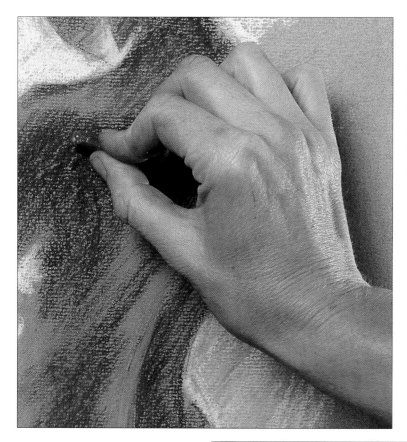

5

Add touches of the same warm red on the model's face, neck and shoulder. Continue developing the flesh tones, deepening the shadow areas with overlaid strokes of dark brown and dark, cold green. Stress the deeper tones by using the side of the pastel stick to make broad marks. Use the same colours on the hair, putting in the shadows that describe the contours of the model's up-swept hairstyle.

6

Add in smooth strokes of pale turquoise green around the figure to give depth and atmosphere to the room. Continue defining the lights and shadows on the model's sarong using both light and dark tones of purple. Then suggest the pattern on the cloth with dark purple, warm red and pale orange.

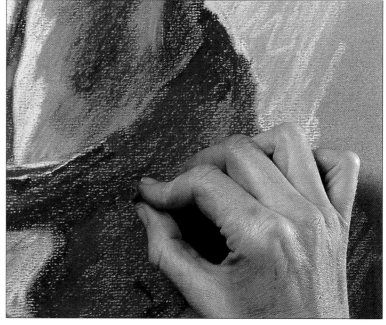

7

Now introduce a little more detail in the background by defining the shuttered window with white, pale blue and pale turquoise green. Draw in the highlights on the model's hair with curving strokes of a pale, soft yellow.

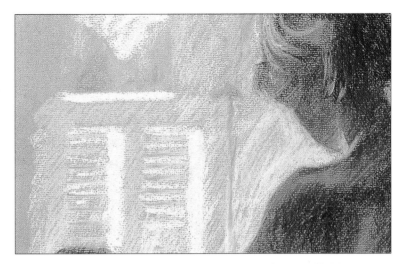

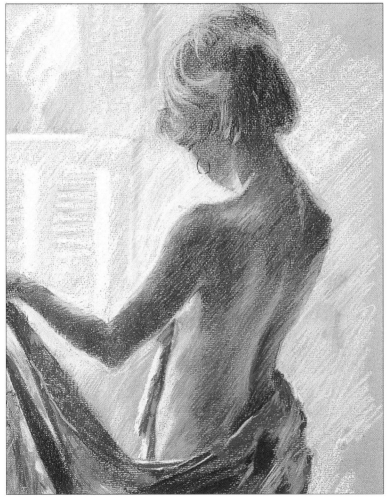

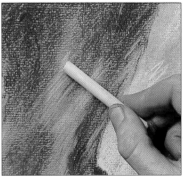

8

Use the same yellow to softly feather over the skin tones to introduce highlights on the model's back and shoulder, with the edge of the pastel stick.

9

With the contours of the figure established, you can now build up the subtle colours in the skin tones with gentle, feathered strokes. Introduce warm yellows and reds on the model's back and arm to create the luminous quality of reflected light and enhance the overall atmosphere of the image. To complete the drawing, add the final details to the pattern on the model's gaily coloured sarong.

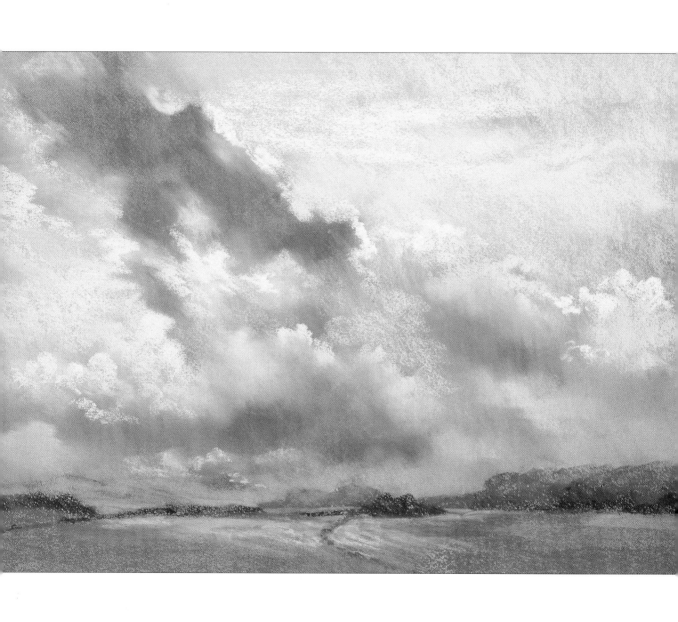

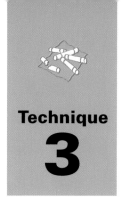

Technique

3

BLENDING

Soft pastels, being powdery, can be smudged and blended very easily to create a range of subtle textures and effects; for example, when suggesting the soft, amorphous nature of skies, water and soft foliage, and in recreating the effects of space, distance and atmosphere.

Blending can give pastel work a sensuous subtlety, but when overdone it creates a slick, "sugary" surface that robs the painting of all character. As a rule of thumb, it is best to retain the textural qualities of the pastel and the surface as much as possible and to use blending selectively and in combination with other, more linear, strokes for contrast.

In this skyscape, the artist did a certain amount of blending with her fingers and with tissues, but most of the soft gradation in the clouds is accomplished by using the pastels on their sides and drifting one colour over another. The surface tooth of the paper breaks up the strokes and forces one to merge with the next, but the colours retain their freshness because they are not degraded by too much rubbing.

Jackie Simmonds
Skyscape
33 x 51cm (13 x 20in)

BLENDING TECHNIQUE

The simplest means of blending consists of laying a patch of solid pastel colour, using the tip or the side of the stick, and fading it gently outward with your finger to create soft tonal gradations. Similarly, two adjoining colours can be blended together where they meet to achieve a gradual colour transition, and two overlaid colours can be blended to create a solid third colour.

The finger is perhaps the most sensitive blending "tool", but depending on the effect you want to achieve, you can use a rag, paper tissue, brush or torchon (a pencil-shaped tube of tightly rolled paper). Use your finger to blend and intensify an area of colour; rags, tissues and brushes to blend large areas and to soften and lift off colour; and a torchon for precise details.

Blending is a very seductive technique, but when overdone it can rob the colours of their freshness and bloom (this bloom is caused by light reflecting off the tiny granules of pigment clinging to the surface of the paper). You don't always have to rub or blend the colours; if you use the pastels on their sides you will find that the gradual overlaying of strokes causes them to merge where required without muddying. A light, unblended application of one colour over another is more vibrant and exciting than a flat area of colour.

It is important to provide visual contrast by integrating blended areas with other, more vigorous pastel strokes. Here, for example, grainy, scumbled strokes give definition to the edges of the clouds.

SKYSCAPE

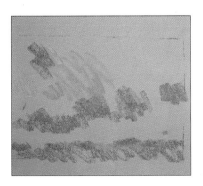

1

With a subject such as a sky, it is best to avoid drawing any outlines, as this could inhibit the freedom of your drawing. Simply plot the main elements of the sky and land using light, scribbled strokes of red-brown, blue-grey, blue-purple and cobalt blue, applied with the sides of the pastels.

Materials and Equipment

• SHEET OF WARM GREY CANSON PAPER • SOFT PASTELS: RED-BROWN, PALE CREAMY YELLOW, PALE ORANGE, BLUE-PURPLE, COBALT BLUE, BLUE-GREY AND LIGHT BLUE-GREY • SOFT TISSUES

2

Use a piece of crumpled soft tissue to soften and blend the pastel marks and remove any excess pastel particles. In effect, you are making a loose underpainting that will enhance the colours you apply on top.

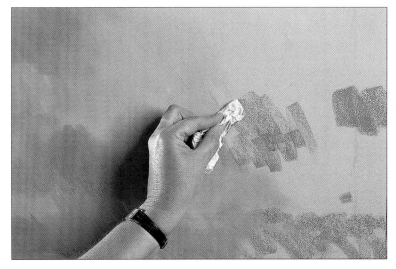

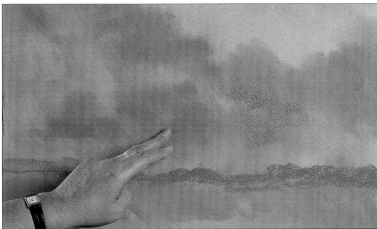

3

With the blue-purple pastel, put in the hills on the distant horizon using side strokes applied with a little more pressure. Start to develop the dark undersides of the cumulus clouds with the same colour, adjusting the pressure on the pastel stick to create denser marks in places. Use your fingers to soften and blur the clouds, dragging the colour downwards to create a sense of movement.

4

Use blue-purple to put in the smaller, flatter clouds near the horizon. This will help to create the illusion of space and recession. Now use a light blue-grey pastel to block in the mid-tones in the clouds, using the same technique used earlier to create the soft, vapourous effect of rain clouds. Adjust the tones by varying the pressure on your fingers as you blend the strokes.

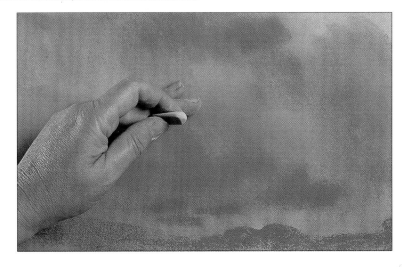

5

Now illuminate the lighter parts of the clouds, and the yellowish tinge of the sky at upper right using a very light tint of creamy yellow. Apply gentle pressure with the side of the pastel stick to float the colour over the grey underlayers.

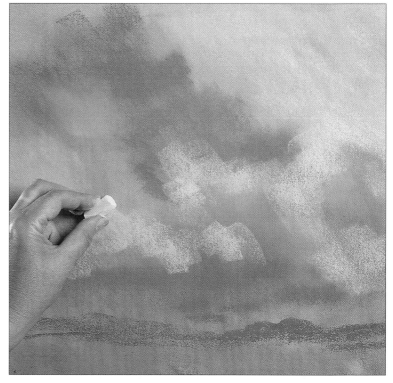

6

Softly blend the creamy yellow tones with your fingers, again using downward strokes. Build up subtle colours in the sky on the right, layering on strokes of pale blue-grey at the top and pale orange along the horizon. Blend a little with your fingers, but leave some of the strokes untouched so that the warm tone of the paper shows through the overlaid colours and enhances the glow of the evening sky.

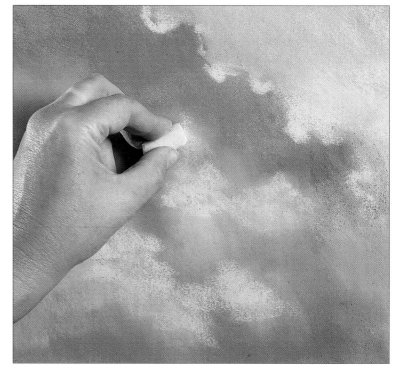

7

Define the sharp, sunlit top edge of the cloud using fairly firm pressure with the tip of the creamy yellow pastel. Then use the same colour to build up the forms of the sunlit tops of the cumulus clouds with small scumbled strokes made by pressing the side of the pastel to the paper and then feathering it away to create soft-edged marks.

8

Build up three-dimensional form in the sunlit clouds by scumbling their top edges and then gently blending the colour downwards with your fingertip as shown, leaving the top edge unblended. The blended strokes create the translucent, airy effect of rain clouds, while the scumbled edges give form and definition, preventing the clouds becoming too "woolly".

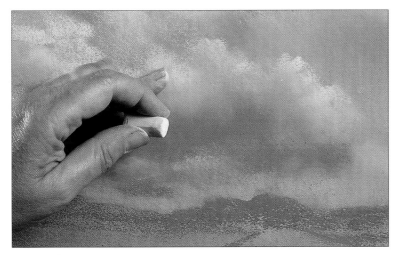

9

As your picture develops, step back from it at intervals to assess the overall effect. Continue to develop the forms within the towering bank of storm cloud, using the tip and side of the creamy yellow pastel to create blended tones and feathered strokes that give the three-dimensional effect of some clouds floating in front of others.

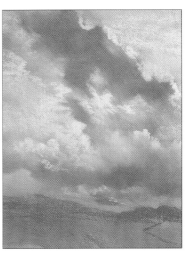

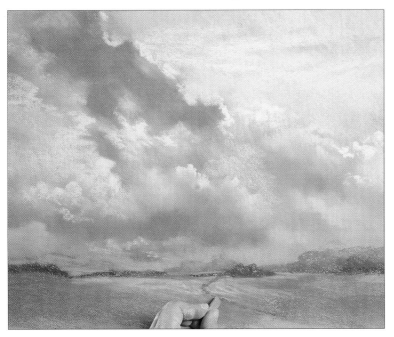

10

Finish the picture by suggesting the forms of the landscape. Go over the distant hills with light blue-grey to push them back in space, then draw in the trees and hedges with the darker blue-grey. For the foreground field, use red-brown modified with overlaid strokes of blue-grey and creamy yellow to suggest patches of light and shadows cast by the clouds. Repeating similar colours in the sky and the land also helps to unify the composition. Use the blue-grey pastel to suggest a curving track through the field that leads the eye into the picture.

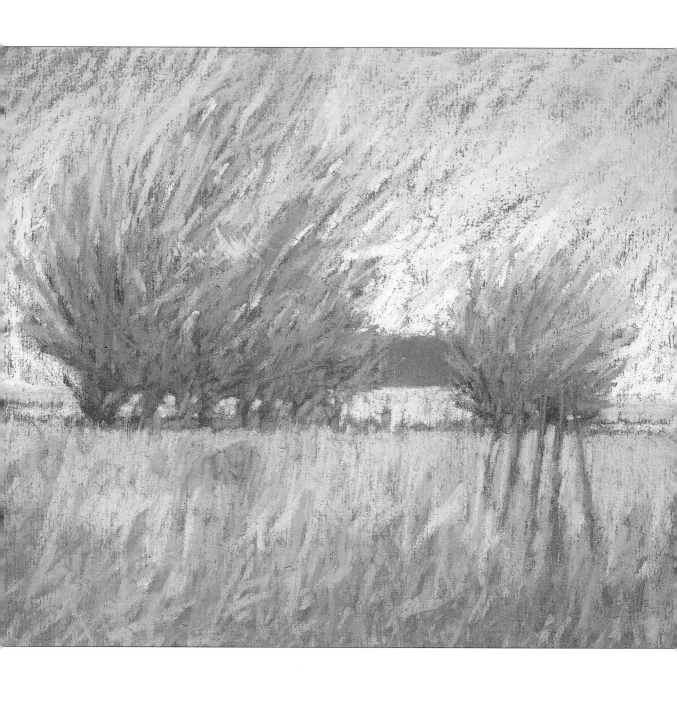

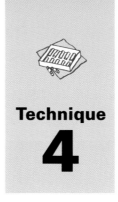

WORKING ON CANVAS

Canvas is an unusual but highly successful surface for pastel painting, especially for the artist who enjoys building up thick layers of colour to create a richly textured "impasto" effect. The heavily toothed surface of canvas is ideal for this technique as it holds a lot of pigment.

This lyrical landscape was painted on stretched canvas, which is a very sympathetic surface to work on. It is taut, but "gives" pleasantly to pressure, and the textured grain enlivens the strokes and gives a surface unity to the work.

The artist began by tinting the canvas with a thin wash of fast-drying acrylic paint in a soft reddish tone that is allowed to break through the pastel marks and provide a counterpoint to the greens laid on top. The underlying tint of the ground acts as a unifying element against which the vibrant pastel colours appear to scintillate.

Barry Freeman
Willow Trees, France
41 x 56cm (16 x 22in)

WORKING ON CANVAS

Cotton and linen canvas, mainly sold for oil painting, can be bought by the metre in larger art stores. They come in different weights and textures; for pastel painting choose a fine to medium grade. Canvas can be stretched taut on a wooden frame or glued onto board using gelatine size or PVA.

Raw, unprimed canvas has a pleasing creamy or brownish tone that provides a sympathetic background for pastel colours. Ready-primed canvas is white, and most pastelists avoid working on a white surface as it gives a false "reading" of the tones and colours applied. Also, the slightly slippery surface of the priming somewhat repels the pastel. These problems are easily overcome by tinting the surface with a thin wash of acrylic or gouache.

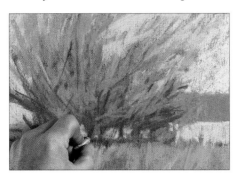

The rough surface tooth of canvas grips the colour well and lends the strokes a broken, grainy appearance. There is enough resistance to the drawn line to make it very pleasant to work on and to give the strokes authority.

WILLOW TREES, FRANCE

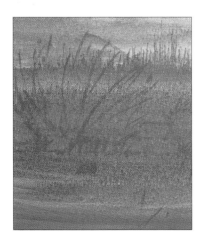

1

Start by tinting the canvas with a soft red ground of acrylic paint. Mix about 70% cadmium red to about 30% cerulean and dilute with water to a thin, "orange juice" consistency. Brush this very loosely over the canvas with a 25mm (1in) decorating brush. There is no need to smooth out the paint – any marks, drips and runs will be covered by the pastel drawing.

Leave to dry, then sketch out the main elements of the composition with a blue-grey pastel.

Materials and Equipment

- SHEET OF STRETCHED CANVAS
- ACRYLICS: CADMIUM RED AND CERULEAN • SOFT PASTELS: VIRIDIAN, MEDIUM HOOKER'S GREEN, SAP GREEN, EMERALD GREEN, OLIVE GREEN, DARK GREEN-BLUE, MEDIUM ULTRAMARINE, DARK ULTRAMARINE, PALE ICY BLUE, LIGHT COBALT BLUE, MEDIUM COBALT BLUE, LIGHT CERULEAN, BLUE-VIOLET, PALE VIOLET, GREY-VIOLET, PALE TURQUOISE BLUE, BLUE-GREY, GREY-GREEN, LIGHT RAW SIENNA, LIGHT BURNT SIENNA, MEDIUM BURNT SIENNA, MADDER BROWN AND MOUSE GREY • 25MM (1IN) DECORATING BRUSH

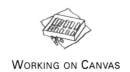
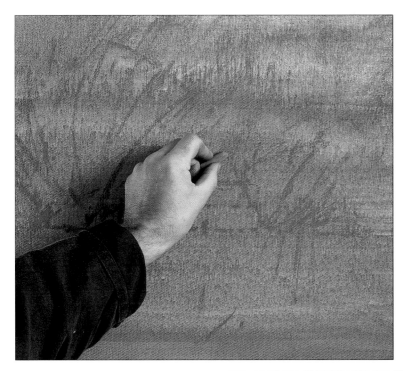

2

Fill the sky area with a medium ultramarine, snapping off a short piece of pastel and using the long edge to lay in loose, diagonal strokes. Notice how the pastel pigment catches on the raised tooth of the canvas. Work lightly at this stage, keeping everything open and workable.

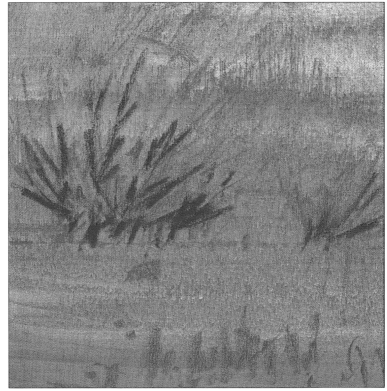

3

Start to suggest the forms of the willow trees with a dark ultramarine and medium Hooker's green, again using the edge of the pastel sticks to make bold linear marks. Work from the base of the trees upwards, to capture the gesture of the wind-tossed branches. Start to sketch in the foreground grasses with Hooker's green.

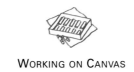

4

Indicate the lighter foliage in the willow trees with strokes of soft grey-green and introduce the same colour into the distant part of the field. Then work into the sky with slashing strokes of light cerulean, cutting into the outlines of the trees. Fill in the grass in the middle ground with strokes of sap green.

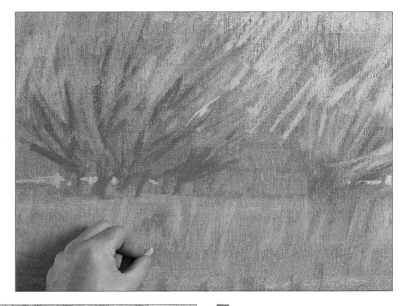

5

Suggest the stone wall of the farmhouse with light raw sienna, leaving small gaps to "read" as the doors and windows. Introduce strokes of pale, icy blue into the lower part of the sky. This cooler blue creates the illusion of receding space in the sky, which always appears warmer in colour at the zenith and gradually becomes cooler nearer the horizon.

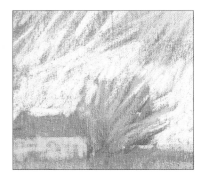

Above: This detail reveals how the canvas breaks up the overlaid pastel strokes, giving them a lively quality. Note also the clever use of complementary colours: the blues in the sky sing out against the warm, orangey-red ground.

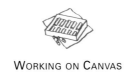
6

Build up the density of tone in the upper part of the sky with a warm, medium cobalt blue, using both the tip and the side of the stick and working the strokes in different directions. Don't attempt to blend the colours but let the strokes drag and mix of their own accord, allowing flecks of the red ground to show through. Bring strokes of the sky colour into the trees to show the gaps between branches.

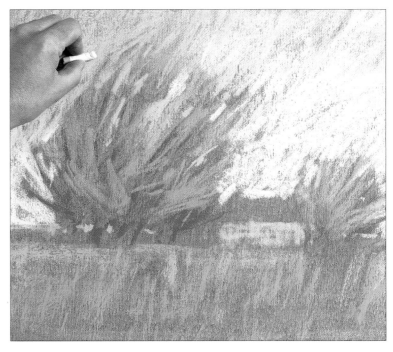

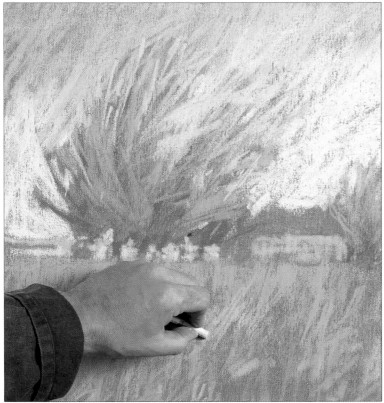

7

Work strokes of light-toned raw sienna into the sky near the horizon. Suggest the landscape glimpsed in the far distance with narrow bands of the same colour, plus light-toned cobalt blue. Use a pale turquoise blue for the silvery, windswept foliage at the tops of the willow trees. Now build up tone and colour in the grassy field in the foreground with strokes of viridian and pale turquoise blue, working around the shape of the grazing cow.

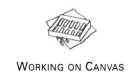
8

Build up a web of shimmering colour in the grassy field with further strokes of medium cobalt blue, viridian, sap green, turquoise and pale raw sienna. Put in the wooden fence posts on the right with strokes of grey-violet. Block in the farmhouse roof with warm madder brown, then work on the trees once more with strokes of pale violet. Use mouse grey for the dark shadows at the base of the trees.

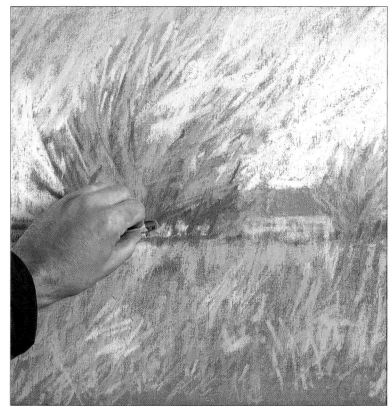

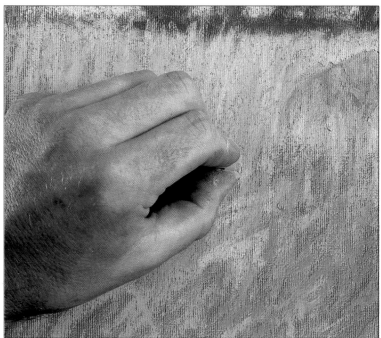

9

Define the form of the grazing cow with angular marks of medium and light tones of burnt sienna. Avoid over-definition, otherwise the animal will appear "pasted on" to the picture. Add strokes of emerald green in the grass, working some strokes over the shape of the cow to link it with the landscape.

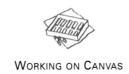
10

Finish off the trees with a network of overlaid strokes of warm and cool greens and blues. Introduce warm olive green into the nearer trees to bring them forward in the picture plane. Add strokes of pale violet on the trunks and lower branches to suggest the cool shadows. Put in small dashes of mouse grey and dark greenish-blue for the shadows under the trees, and suggest the cast shadow on the farmhouse roof with more pale violet.

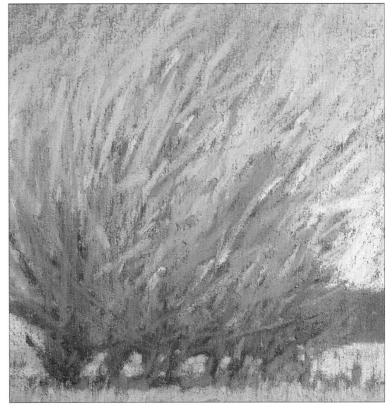

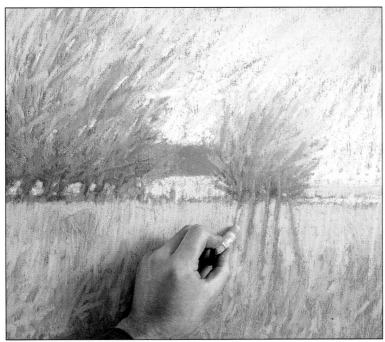

11

Step back from your picture and assess the overall balance of tone and colour. Finish off the grass, adding bold strokes of viridian and emerald green in the immediate foreground and leaving some of the red undertone visible. To create the illusion of receding space, use smaller strokes and cool grey-green for the grass at the back of the field. Finally, put in the highlights on the fence posts with light burnt sienna and blue-violet.

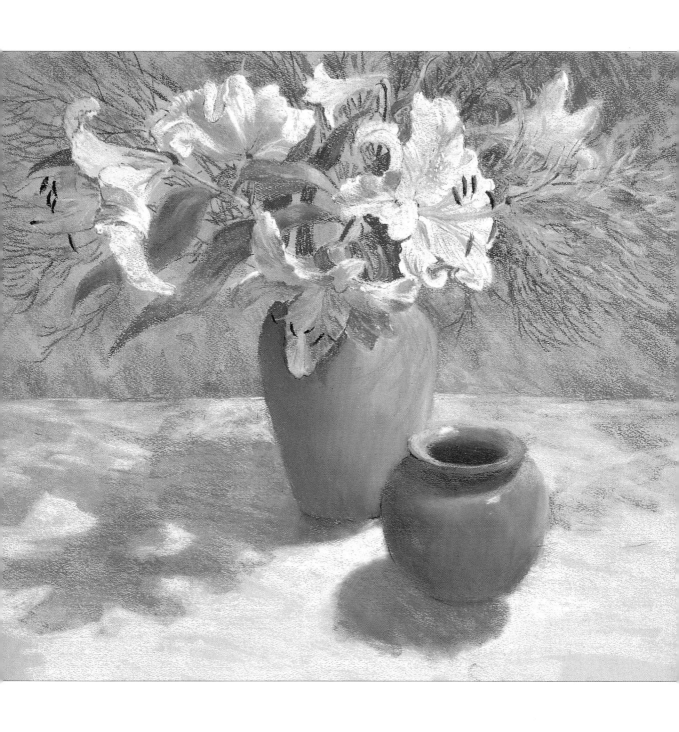

Technique

5

USING COLOURED GROUNDS

Few pastelists work on white paper. There are two reasons for this, the first being that the bright, intense hues of pastel are not shown to their best advantage on white paper, appearing rather dark, whereas they seem to sparkle on a toned paper. Secondly, because the grainy texture of pastel usually allows the colour of the paper to show through and between the applied pastel strokes, patches of white paper glaringly "jump out", ruining the effect of the picture and devaluing the applied colours, whereas a coloured ground becomes an integral part of the image and exerts a subtle influence on the colours laid over it.

The cool tonality of this elegant still life is enhanced by the choice of a neutral grey paper, which serves as the basis for the shadow tones. The artist has left small glints of untouched paper visible that allow the applied colours to "breathe", maintaining the unique airiness and sparkle that makes a pastel painting so attractive.

~

Jackie Simmonds
White Lilies
47 x 57cm (18½ x 22½in)

~

WORKING ON COLOURED GROUNDS

With pastels, perhaps more than with any other drawing medium, the colour of the support plays a crucial role. This is because pastel pigments sit on the surface of the paper rather than staining it as paints do. Light strokes applied to a rough surface will give a broken texture, and when two different pastel colours are laid lightly one over the other so that the paper shows through, the paper acts as a third colour.

It makes sense, therefore, to choose paper of a colour that will make a positive contribution to the overall colour scheme of the painting. You may, for example, wish to select a paper that is similar in tone or colour to the subject and provides an overall middle tone, so all that is needed to complete the painting are the highlights and shadows. Alternatively, you could choose a light-toned paper, which would serve as the highlight areas, or a dark-toned one, which would provide the shadow areas.

Think about the mood and tonality of the subject, then decide whether you want the background colour to complement or contrast with it. For example, when painting a summer landscape you might choose a soft green paper that acts as one of the key foliage colours and enhances the luminosity of the subject. On the other hand, you might choose a warm earth colour that complements the greens and makes them appear more vibrant.

By allowing the colour of the support to play an integral part in the painting, you achieve two things. First, when small patches of the paper's colour are glimpsed between the overlaid pastel strokes, it becomes a unifying element, tying together the colours laid over it.

Second, you can actually get away with putting fewer marks on the paper, and this gives an attractive freshness and immediacy to the finished painting. When painting trees, for example, a few brief strokes of colour applied over a contrasting paper will "read" as dense foliage, without risk of overworking the image.

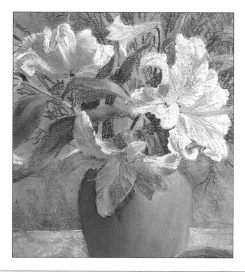

When glimpses of the bare paper are allowed to show through the areas of pastel they emphasize the "bite" – the directions and edges of the strokes – and give a lively working feel.

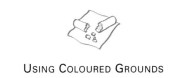

WHITE LILIES

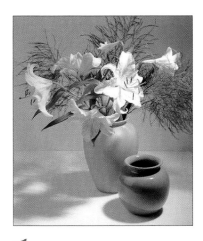

Left Spectacular white lilies form the focal point of this still-life group, with its harmonious colour scheme of cool white, blues and greens.

Materials and Equipment

- SHEET OF GREY CANSON PAPER
- SOFT PASTELS: RED-BROWN, ORANGE, PALE CREAM, LEMON YELLOW, YELLOW-GREEN, MEDIUM LEAF GREEN, LIGHT VIRIDIAN, PALE TURQUOISE, MEDIUM TURQUOISE, MEDIUM COBALT BLUE, MEDIUM PRUSSIAN BLUE, GREEN-GREY, BLUE-GREY, GREY-PURPLE AND WHITE • STICK OF FINE CHARCOAL • STICK OF WHITE CHALK

1

Working on the smooth side of the paper, lightly sketch the main outlines of the group with charcoal, dividing the picture area into interesting shapes. Drawing vertical lines down the centres of the vase and pot will help you to draw their shapes accurately. Use white chalk to indicate the light tones. Gently flick the charcoal lines with a rag to knock them back.

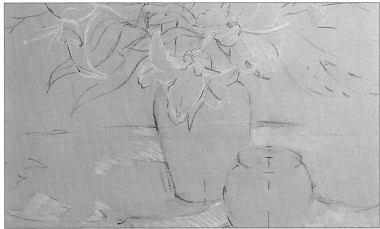

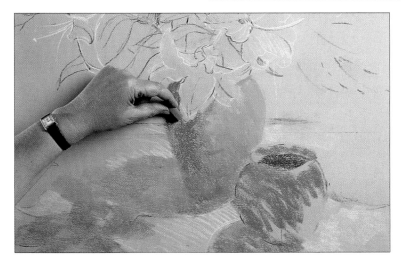

2

Start by placing a few strokes of local colour around to emphasize the shapes and indicate the tonal values of the picture. Work lightly, using broken pieces of pastel on their sides. Use a medium-toned cobalt blue for the jug, with Prussian blue inside the rim. For the vase, plot the light, medium and dark tones with a light viridian green, green-grey and medium turquoise, respectively. Bring the colour of each object down into its shadow so that the two shapes are linked. Float strokes of blue-grey and grey-purple over these shadows, to suggest the shadows cast by the lilies.

3

Block in the background behind the group with very light side strokes of grey-purple, then use the same colour to put in the shadows on the lilies. (Squint at the flowers through half-closed eyes so that you can see the dominant lights and darks more clearly.)

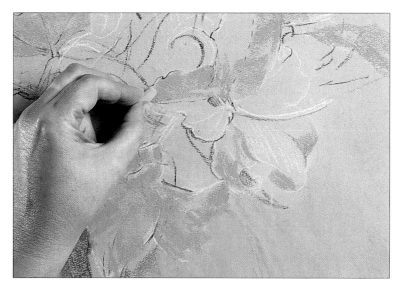

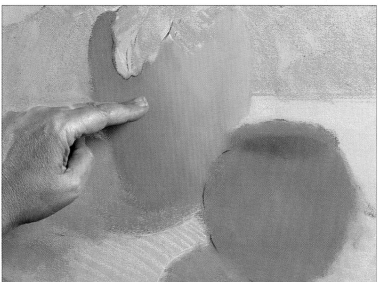

4

Use your fingertips to work over the colours applied to the vase and pot until they are blended into continuous gradations that describe their rounded forms. These soft tones also suggest the matt surface of the porcelain. Apply a light spray of fixative to the painting so that the light colours you add later will sit on top of those underneath rather than mixing with them.

5

Use a very pale cream pastel to put in the highlights on the lilies and on the table, and add hints of lemon yellow on the trumpets of the lilies. Move lightly over the paper so that its colour maintains a strong presence, glinting through the overlaid strokes.

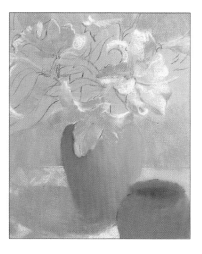

6

Now block in the leaves and stalks on the lilies, first putting in the darkest tones with a medium leafy green. Apply the colour lightly, with gentle side strokes, so as not to overload the grain of the paper with colour.

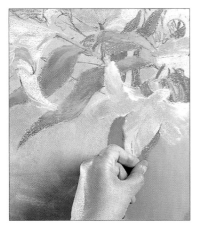

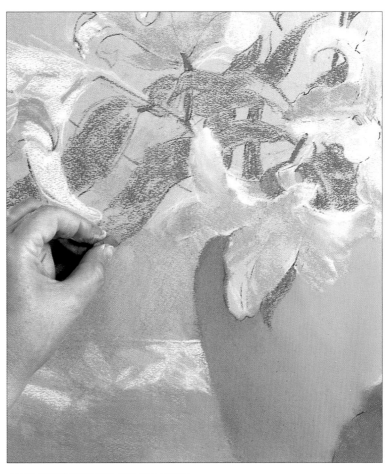

7

Use the same green, this time using the tip of the pastel, to suggest the feathery ferns that fan out between the lilies. Then add the highlights on the lily leaves and stalks with a warm, yellowy green.

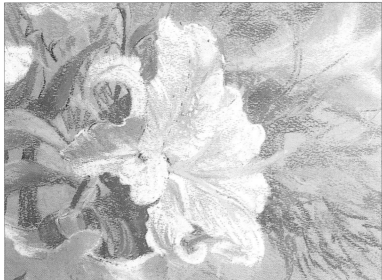

8

Now start to develop the lights on the lily flowers with white and very pale cream. Use the tip or edge of the pastels now, and apply a little more pressure. The lily at the front forms the focal point of the group, so concentrate detail here by suggesting the slightly raised texture of the petals with lines and dots. Allow glints of grey paper to show through, representing the cool, delicate shadows on the flowers. Draw the long stamens lightly with yellow-green.

9

Gently brush delicate hints of pale turquoise and grey-purple onto the shadowy undersides of the flowers, again letting the grey paper show through. Highlight the frilly edges on some of the petals with white pastel.

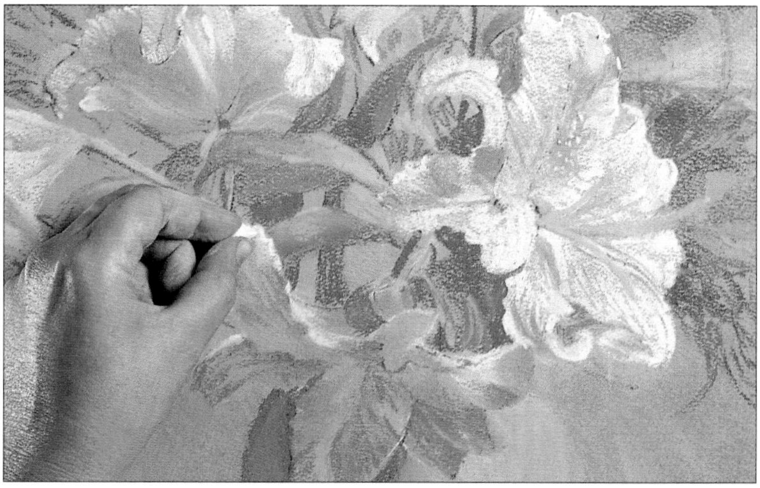

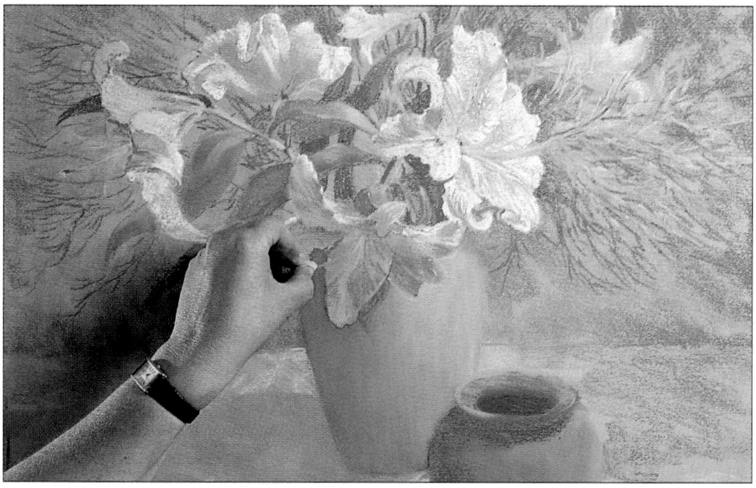

10

Don't work on one area for too long but move around the painting, adjusting the tones in relation to their neighbours. Add further strokes of grey-purple in the background, then develop the form of the blue pot by adding the shadow on the left with Prussian blue and the highlight on the rim with pale cream. Develop the foliage further with yellow-green, and put in the stamens on the lilies.

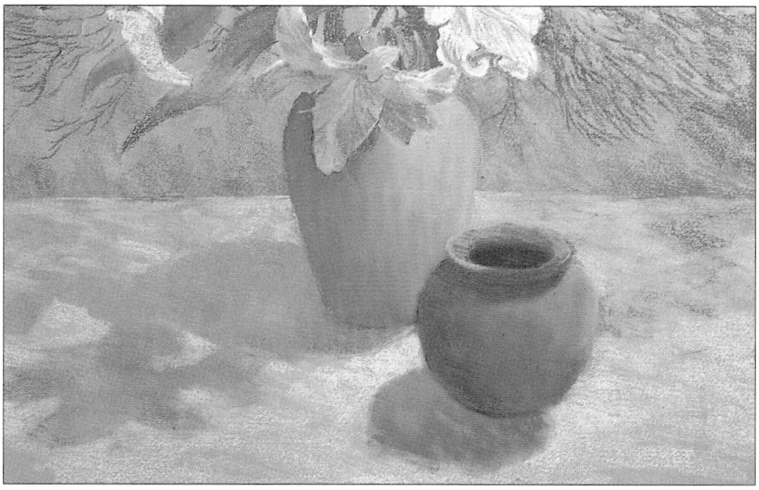

11

Now work on the table top, using delicate side strokes of pale cream to describe the patterns of dappled light that fall between the cast shadows of the flowers. Float the colour on gently, using the broad side of the pastel, so that the cool grey of the paper glints through.

12

Apply soft strokes of pale turquoise and leaf green to the vase to suggest the dappled shadows and highlights cast onto it by the foliage. Use your fingertip to blend and graduate the tones on the blue pot to show how light describes its three-dimensional form. Then add the orange stripe on the rim of the pot and build up thick strokes of pure white for the bright highlights.

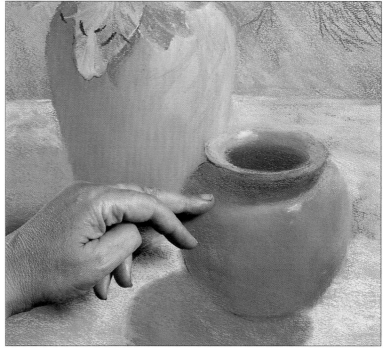

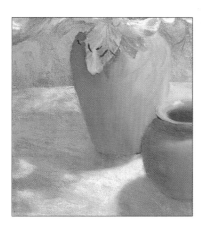

13

Now add just a whisper of cobalt blue to the shadows on the table to make them more luminous. To anchor the vase and pot to the table, slightly darken the area of shadow directly beneath them. Then use your fingertip to very gently soften the edges of the shadows.

14

Finally, add the pollen-covered anthers at the ends of the flower stamens using red-brown, overlaid with touches of orange.

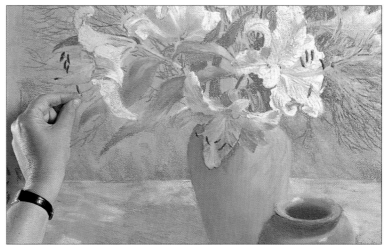

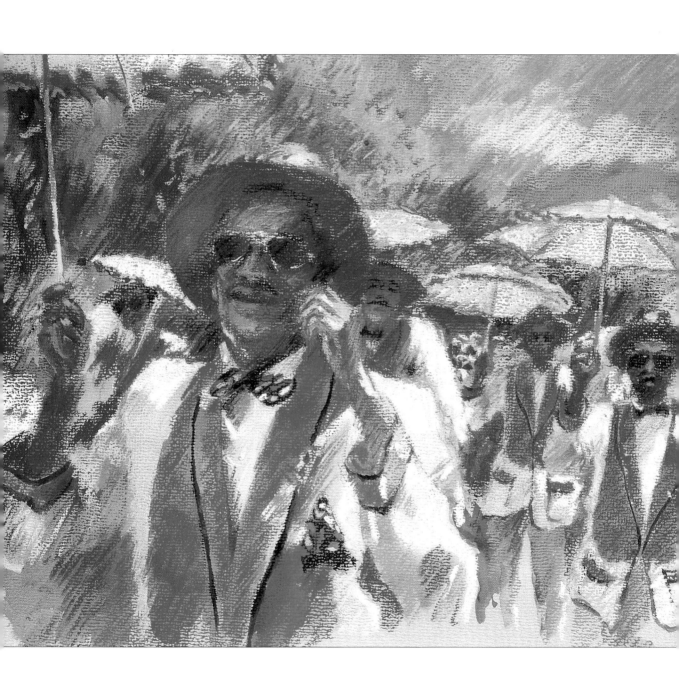

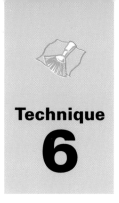

MIXED MEDIA

Because pastel is such a flexible medium it can be combined successfully with other drawing and painting media to create optical and textural effects that will broaden the range and expressiveness of your paintings. By combining pastel with an aqueous medium such as watercolour, gouache or acrylic, for example, you can exploit the unique qualities of each medium and use them to enhance each other.

In this lively painting the fluid, translucent quality of watercolour makes a perfect foil for the opaque, splattered, scintillating qualities of the overlaid pastel strokes. The artist began by blocking in the composition with watercolour washes to establish the main colour areas and the patterns of light and shade. When the watercolour was dry, she reworked the image in loose, grainy pastel strokes to develop detail and emphasize colour accents and tonal contrasts. Where the painted areas break through in places a striking optical effect is created with the pastel overpainting.

Hazel Soan
Mardi Gras
33 x 38cm (13 x 15in)

USING MIXED MEDIA

Aside from the aesthetic considerations, there are also some practical advantages to combining pastel with paint media. First, aqueous media can cover large areas quickly while still leaving enough surface tooth for the subsequent layers of pastel to adhere to. This enables you to establish correctly patterns of lights and darks, to lay a kind of blueprint of complementary colours and tones to be later deepened or lightened with pastel, to work out compositional problems, and to avoid the dense and overworked appearance that might result from building up too many layers of pastel.

Second, the one complaint artists have about pastels is that it is difficult to create really rich, dark tones with them – there are far fewer dark pastels than light ones, and even the deepest shades tend to come up relatively light on application. This problem can be overcome by first blocking in the dark areas of the composition with paint to give them more strength.

When using water-based media with pastel the paper must be strong enough to take the wetting. This means you must either mount your paper on a stiff cardboard backing, or use heavy watercolour paper (at least 285gsm/140lb).

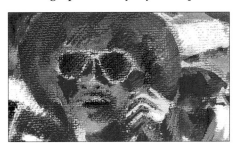

This detail reveals how the surface grain of watercolour paper breaks up the pastel colours, giving a speckled effect that provides a lively contrast with the watercolour washes beneath.

MARDI GRAS

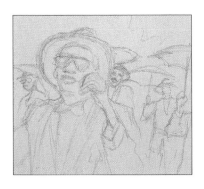

1

Sketch out the figures with an HB pencil. Pay particular attention to the proportions of the figures and the way they diminish in scale in the distance.

Materials and Equipment

• SHEET OF BEIGE CANSON PAPER • WATERCOLOURS: PERMANENT ROSE, CERULEAN, FRENCH ULTRAMARINE, BURNT SIENNA AND SCARLET LAKE • SOFT PASTELS: PALE PINK, MAGENTA, BRIGHT YELLOW, YELLOW-GREEN, YELLOW OCHRE, CERULEAN, DARK BLUE-GREEN, MEDIUM GREEN, TURQUOISE, COBALT BLUE, BURNT SIENNA, BLACK AND WHITE • MEDIUM-SIZE ROUND WATERCOLOUR BRUSH • HB PENCIL

2

Mix up a wash of permanent rose and apply this over all the areas of the picture that are to be warm in colour, such as the darker flesh tones and the musicians' pink jackets. Use a medium-size round brush and apply the paint freely and intuitively across the paper.

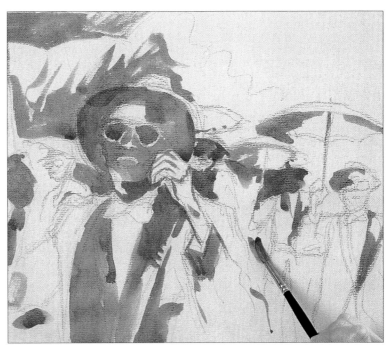

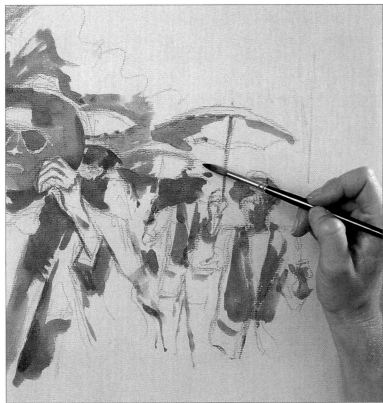

3

Now mix a wash of cerulean and use this to sketch in the cool, shadowy undertones. Again, work freely and rapidly rather than attempting to "fill in" specific areas.

4

Brush in the sky area on the right with a loose wash of burnt sienna. This will provide a warm undertone for the cool pastel colours applied over it later. Apply touches of burnt sienna elsewhere around the composition to provide colour echoes that will help to unify the whole picture.

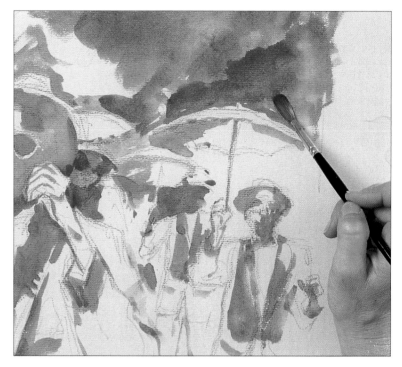

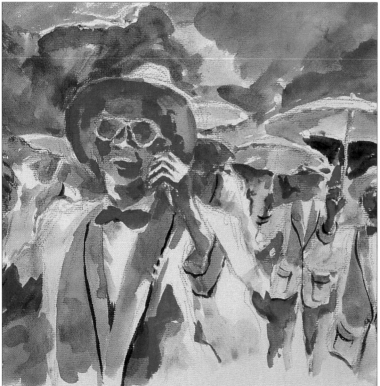

5

Finally, mix a wash of scarlet lake and use this to define the deepest tones, such as the cast shadows on the face of the foreground figure. Leave touches of bare paper showing to serve as the brightest highlights. Mix French ultramarine and permanent rose and sketch in the detailing on the musicians' jackets using the tip of the brush. Now leave the painting to dry.

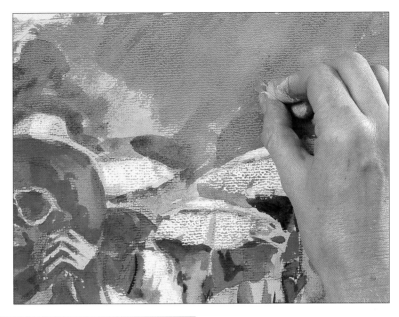

6

Snap off a short length of cerulean pastel and work over the sky area with the side of the stick. Apply gentle pressure so that the colour deposits only on the peaks of the paper grain, allowing the burnt sienna wash underneath to show through the pastel strokes.

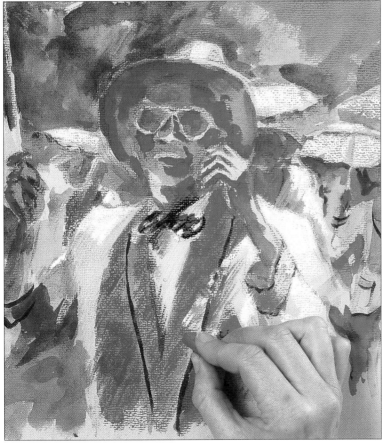

7

Now work on the foreground figure, filling in the pattern on the bow tie with dots of black, white and yellow pastel. Work over the pink parts of the jacket with parallel hatched strokes of pale pink and bright magenta.

8

Apply strokes of white pastel over the light areas of the foreground musician's jacket. Then lightly hatch over the shadow under the brim of his hat with cobalt blue. The interaction of the warm pink underwashes and the cool blue pastel strokes sets up a vibrant effect that captures the sensation of bright sunlight.

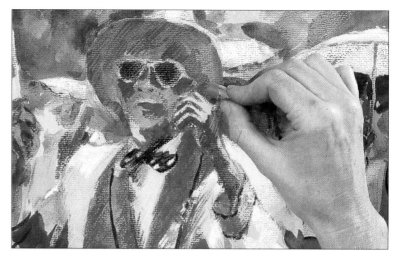

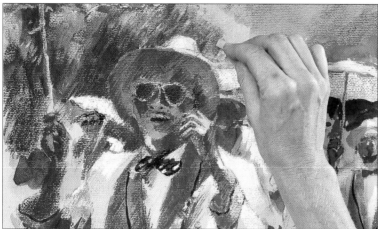

9

Add strokes of burnt sienna and yellow ochre on the musician's face and arms, then accentuate the shadows on his face with cobalt blue. Go over the sunglasses with black, then define the mouth and moustache. Fill in the parasol at top left with blended strokes of pink and white. Now move on to the trees in the background, indicating clumps of foliage with dark blue-green, medium green and light yellow-green. Note how the undertone of burnt sienna adds depth and richness to these greens.

10

Continue working around the composition, building up tone and detail and gradually bringing the picture into focus. Fill in the parasols with white, edged with cobalt blue, then deepen the tones on the left of the picture.

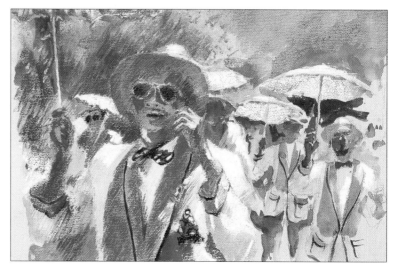

11

Now start to work on the figures in the background. Jot in the musicians' facial features and sunglasses with black, then shade the underbrims of the hats with cobalt blue. Fill in the jackets with hatched strokes of white and magenta.

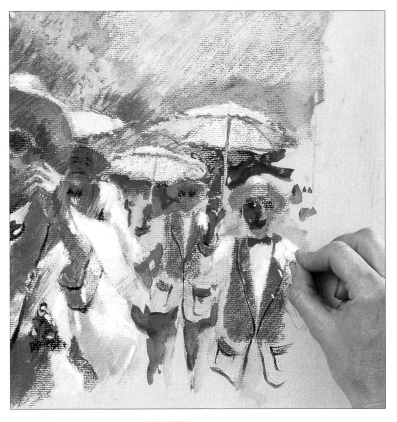

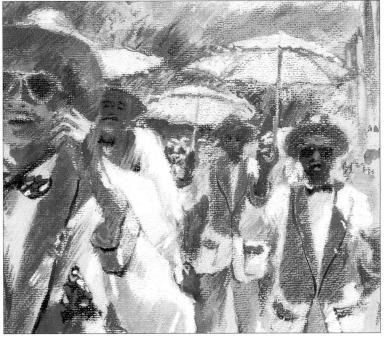

12

Complete the jackets and trousers on the background figures with strokes of turquoise, letting the watercolour tints break through the overlaid pastel strokes. Fill in the hats with cobalt blue and white. Finally, give more definition to the facial features of the righthand figure using bright yellow, black and pale pink. Leave the other figures relatively undefined as they are farther back in space.

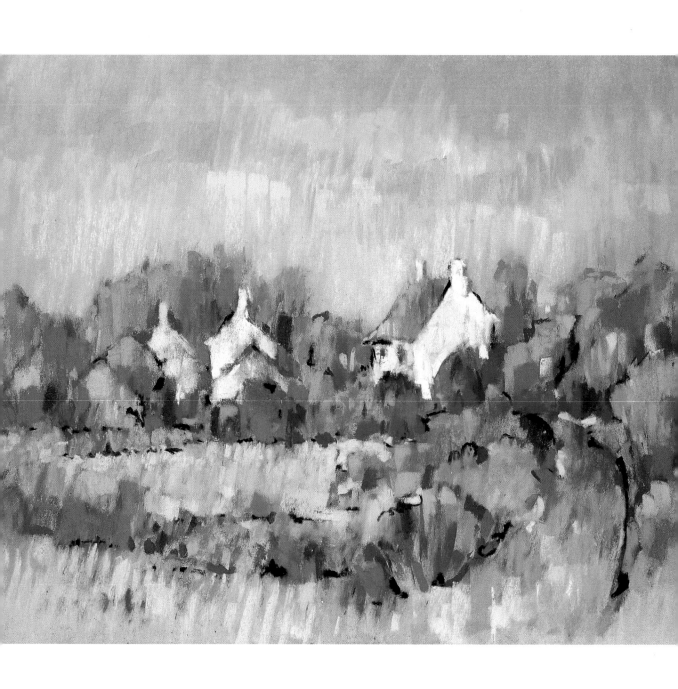

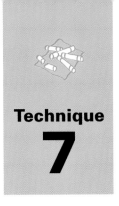

Technique
7

EXPRESSIVE STROKES

Pastels are unique in the way they combine the properties of drawing and painting media, providing rich qualities of colour and texture as well as a sensitive line quality. They also offer the satisfaction of immediate contact with the paper; variations between line and mass are instinctively wrought through the natural movements of the hand and the pastel stick.

The marks you can make with pastel are infinitely variable, as is amply demonstrated in this colourful landscape painting. The artist has worked on glasspaper, an abrasive, heavily toothed surface that enables him to apply layer upon layer of rich, dense colour. Using small, broken pieces of pastel, he gradually built up the colour density with broad drifts and grainy, open-textured side strokes, occasionally dashing in brilliant colour accents. He was careful to keep the whole surface active at every stage, letting the painting grow naturally and "talk back" as it progressed.

Geoff Marsters
Near St. Jacques, Brittany
37 x 49cm (14½ x 19in)

MAKING EXPRESSIVE MARKS

Each of us has a handwriting style that is unique and personal to us alone. Whether our writing is neat and precise, or full of flamboyant curves and loops, it unconsciously expresses something of our personality. The same thing applies to art; every line and stroke an artist puts into a drawing or painting expresses something about that artist as well as his or her subject. A classic example of this is to be found in the violent, swirling lines in the work of Vincent van Gogh (1853–1890), which express the intensity of his emotions and the tortured state of his mind.

Pastel sticks can be broken to produce a range of different marks and edge qualities. With practice, the differ-

ent ways of manipulating the pastel – switching from tip to side and varying the pressure – will become second nature and your own personal "handwriting" will begin to emerge. Working with the long side of the pastel creates broad, painterly strokes that can be swept in as grainy "washes". Working with the tip of the crayon, or a broken edge, you can make thin lines and crisp strokes or rough dabs and dashes that create an altogether different feel. Add to this the different effects achieved by combining soft and hard pastels, rough and smooth papers, and different coloured papers, and you will begin to see why pastel is such an expressive and fascinating medium to work with.

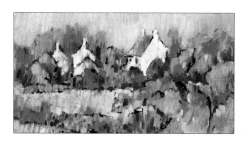

Pastel sticks can be broken to produce a range of different marks and edge qualities that act descriptively and lend vitality to an image.

NEAR ST. JACQUES, BRITTANY

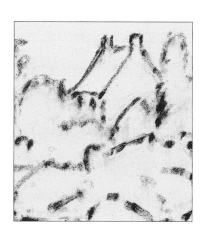

1

Mark out the composition using a deep shade of ultramarine (if you doubt your drawing abilities, make light charcoal outlines first and then go over them with pastel). Let the pastel stick dance over the paper, creating lively, broken lines rather than solid, continuous ones.

Materials and Equipment

• SHEET OF FINE GRADE GLASSPAPER • SOFT PASTELS: PALE PINK, RUST RED, BRIGHT ORANGE, ORANGE-BROWN, SOFT YELLOW, GOLDEN YELLOW, LIGHT GREEN, DARK GREEN, VIBRANT GREEN, ULTRAMARINE DEEP, TURQUOISE BLUE, COBALT BLUE, MAUVE, VIBRANT BLUE, PURPLE-GREY, PALE OCHRE, WHITE AND BLACK • SOFT TISSUES

2

Assess the main shadow areas in the subject and then block them in, using a short piece of purple-grey pastel on its side to stroke the colour on lightly.

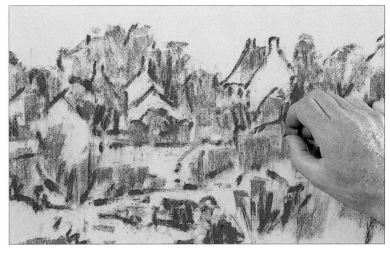

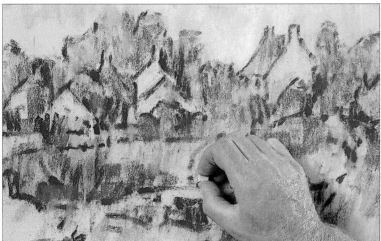

3

Start to define the light/dark accents in the landscape, putting in the lighter tones with strokes of cobalt blue and mauve. Move lightly over the paper so as not to fill up the grain too quickly.

4

Continue applying soft strokes of mauves, pinks, yellows and orangey browns in the sky. Introduce the same colours into the landscape to link the two together and unify the picture. At this stage you are not too concerned with depicting objects but concentrating on getting a flow of colour moving through the composition.

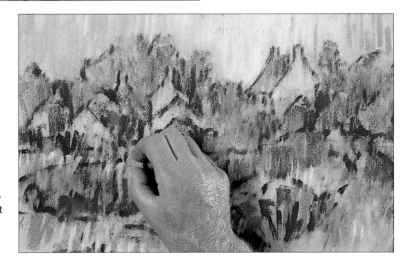

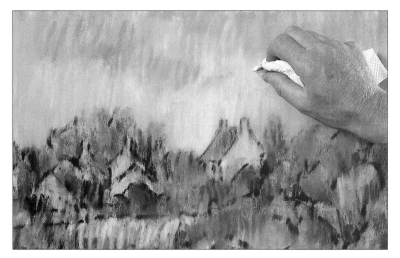

5

Introduce some strokes of light, cool green into the landscape. Get rid of any excess pastel dust on the surface of the picture by holding the board at a vertical angle and tapping it lightly onto a piece of newspaper. When you are satisfied with the distribution of colours and tones in the composition, work across the picture with a piece of crumpled tissue, very gently smudging the colours and softening the strokes. Work in a vertical direction.

6

Build up more colour in the sky with vertical strokes of pale pink, mauve and yellow, plus touches of white and light green. Use gentle pressure to create soft veils of colour, and bring the strokes down into the tops of the trees so that sky and land are linked. These broken strokes of high-key colour recreate the scintillating, sparkling effect of light in the sky.

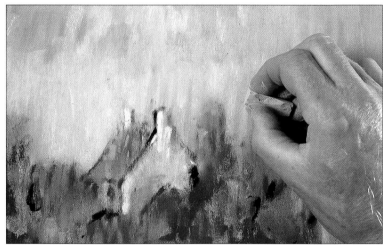

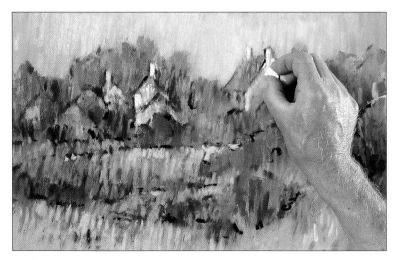

7

Now bring some warm colour into the landscape, to echo the warm yellowy hues in the sky. Use the tip of a golden yellow pastel to make short, vertical marks, applying more pressure now. Use these bright hues as visual "stepping stones", arranging them in subtle lines and curves that encourage the eye to explore the composition. Start to fill in the white walls of the houses, which are the focal point of the composition.

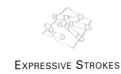

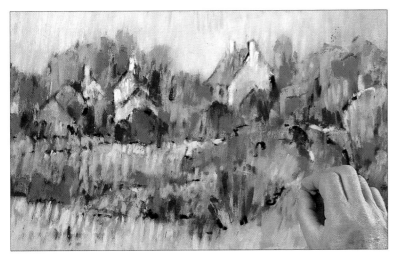

8

Build up stronger hues in the landscape, bringing in rich touches of vibrant blue, bright orange and rusty red. Use the tip and the side of the pastel sticks to create a varied range of marks, some linear and some broad and blocky.

9

Strengthen the whites on the buildings to make them stand out. Now bring in small strokes and flecks of rich turquoise blue and vibrant green, once again using these points of strong colour to reinforce the rhythms and movement in the composition.

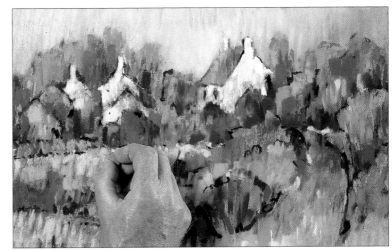

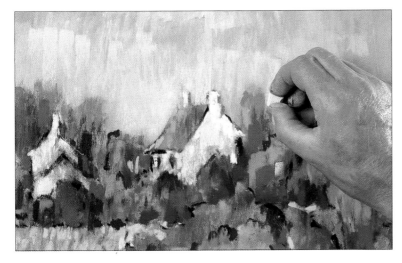

10

Complete the painting by feathering soft strokes of pale ochre in the sky near the horizon. Add small touches in the landscape as well, to unify and harmonize the picture. Do not spray-fix the completed painting because this would darken and alter the colour values. Store the picture carefully and frame it behind glass as soon as possible.

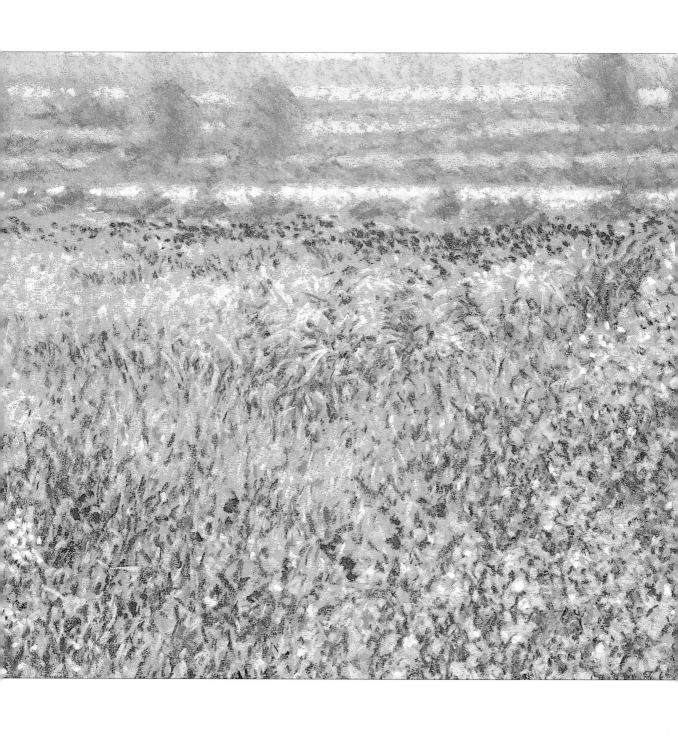

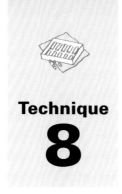

Technique

8

POINTILLISM

The French painters Georges Seurat (1859–1891) and Paul Signac (1863–1935) developed the pointillist technique towards the end of the nineteenth century, using oil paints. Evolving from the Impressionists' use of broken colour, pointillism involves creating an image from hundreds of tiny dots of pure colour. Seen from the appropriate viewing distance, these dots "read" as a coherent surface and the colours take on a luminous quality.

Pointillism in its pure form is a very exacting technique, but it doesn't have to be applied methodically – used in a free and spontaneous manner it produces sparkling colours and a lively and entertaining surface.

Pastels are particularly suited to the pointillist technique because of their pure, vibrant hues and ease of manipulation. In this impressionistic painting the many touches of colour add a shimmering quality to the surface, making it dance and vibrate. The poppies are picked out with quick, dashing strokes and stippled dots that make no attempt to shape the flowers, but are simply notes of colour. Small patches of the buff-coloured paper remain exposed throughout the picture, the warm colour giving an underlying unity to the mass of pastel strokes and enhancing the effect of sunlight.

Derek Daniells
Poppy Field
33 x 41cm (13 x 16in)

POINTILLIST TECHNIQUE

The technique of pointillism involves building up an image with small dots and flecks of pure colour that are not joined but leave some of the toned support showing through. When seen from the normal viewing distance, these dots appear to merge into one mass of colour, but the effect is more vibrant than that created by a solid area of blended colour. Because each dot is separate, the colours appear to shimmer and sparkle, and this is due to the way in which tiny dots of colour vibrate on the retina of the eye.

If complementary (opposite) colours are juxtaposed, the effect is even more pronounced. For example, when dots of red and green, or yellow and violet,

are intermixed, the colours are mutually enhanced by contrast and the effect is strikingly vibrant. However, it is important to note that this vibrancy is only achieved when the colours are similar in tone.

The aim of this technique is to achieve a sense of immediacy; the colours should be applied rapidly and confidently and then left with no attempt made to blend them together. Try to vary the size, shape and density of the marks you make, otherwise the effect will be monotonous. By altering the pressure applied, you can make a range of stippled dots and broken flecks and dabs that give life and energy to the image.

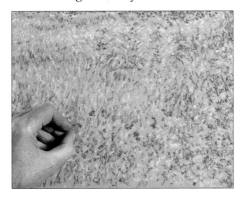

Successful optical mixing depends on spacing the colours well in the early stages, leaving enough room to build up the succeeding colours.

POPPY FIELD

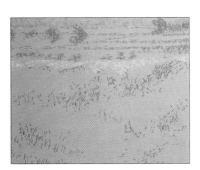

1

This image is based on a loose build-up of strokes, so avoid drawing outlines as they restrict your mark-making. Plot the structure of the work with small, widely spaced marks, using pale tints of ultramarine and mauve for the sky, sap green and cadmium yellow for the fields, and green-grey for the grasses.

Materials and Equipment

• SHEET OF BUFF-COLOURED PASTEL PAPER • SOFT PASTELS: CADMIUM YELLOW, SAP GREEN, OLIVE GREEN, GREEN-GREY, VERMILION, WHITE, AND VERY PALE TINTS OF ULTRAMARINE BLUE, MAUVE, VIRIDIAN, OCHRE AND CERULEAN

2

Define the horizontal lines of the distant fields and the shadow sides of the trees with ultramarine. Then work on the wild-flower field with small flicks and strokes, using very light tints of mauve, viridian, cadmium yellow and ochre. Touch in the colours very gently, keeping the pastel marks loosely spaced.

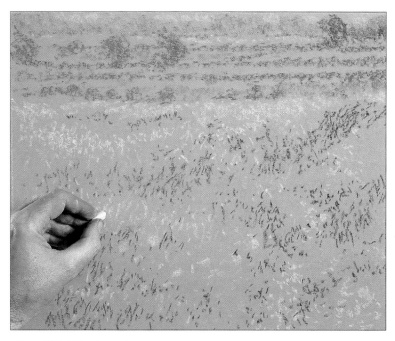

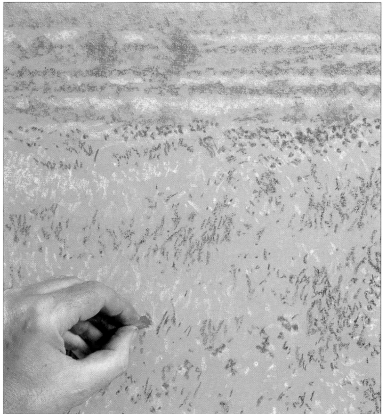

3

Suggest sunlight streaking across the distant fields with a couple of light, broken, horizontal lines of viridian. Keep adding touches of colour over the whole image, letting your pastels "dance" over the paper and keeping the whole surface active. Spot in some vermilion for the poppies, applying it over the yellow marks already made.

4

Indicate the light tones in the sky with very pale cerulean and white. Touch in warm sap green on the left side of the trees, to give them three-dimensional form and to indicate the direction of the light. Add lines of very pale ochre to suggest cornfields in the distance.

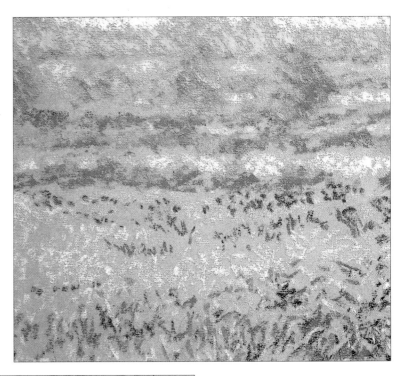

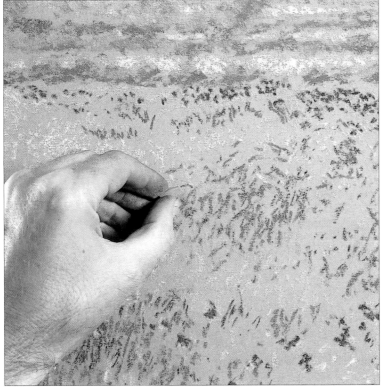

5

Flick in the tops of the grasses with sap green, varying the direction of the strokes to describe how they bend in the breeze. If all the strokes run in the same direction, the effect looks more like rain than grass!

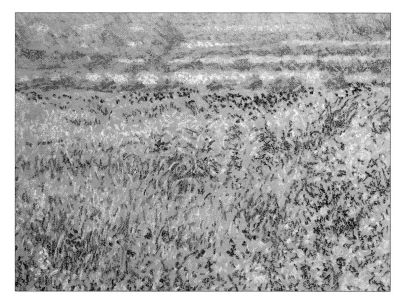

6

Continue patiently building up the textures and forms of the foreground grasses and flowers. Move lightly over the paper so that its warm colour maintains a strong presence, glinting through the overlaid strokes. Use the same colours as before, with the addition of olive green to give warmth to the shadowy grasses and touches of white to give sparkle to the blue flowers.

7

Step back to assess your progress, then make necessary adjustments. Here, the artist feels that the tone of the trees is too strong so he lightly strokes mauve over them. This "knocks back" the colour, pushing the trees back in space. The thin veil of mauve also gives the impression of hazy summer afternoon light.

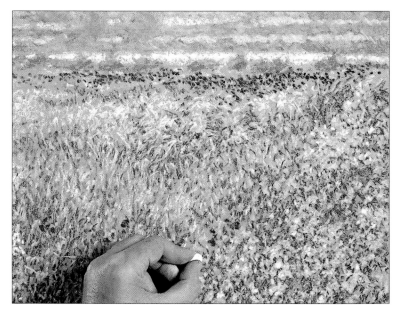

8

Gradually build up the density of marks in the foreground with small strokes and flecks worked in different directions. Concentrate more detail on the flowers in the foreground to bring them forward in the picture plane, thus accentuating the feeling of space in the background landscape.

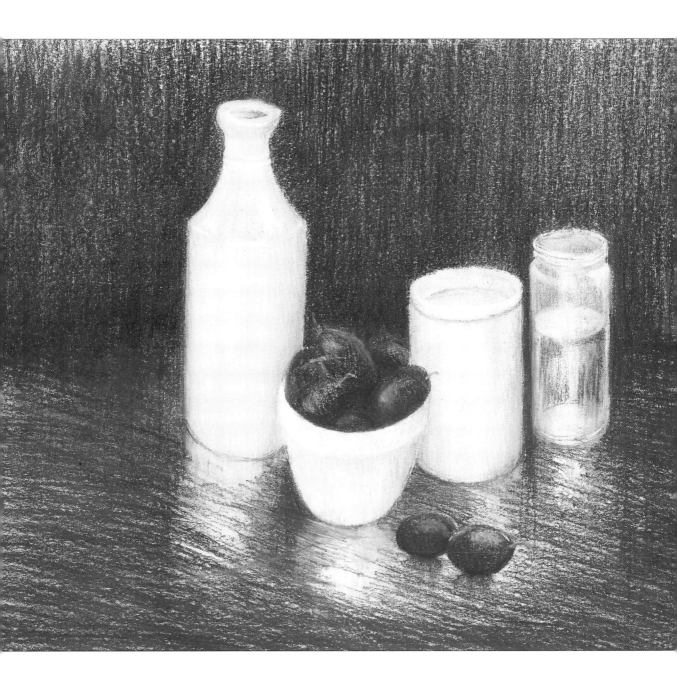

HATCHING AND CROSSHATCHING

There are many different ways of "mixing" pastel colours on the paper surface. By using the hatching technique of laying a series of roughly parallel lines in different colours or tones it is possible to achieve an optical mixing effect with the lines merging to give the impression of continuous colour.

This still-life study is a good example of the complexity of colour and tone that can be achieved with hatching and cross-hatching. The artist has woven subtle and complex hues from a series of densely packed parallel lines worked mostly in a vertical direction. Seen from the appropriate viewing distance, these linear marks "read" as a coherent surface, while at a closer view the colour interactions and lively textural qualities of the mingled strokes can be appreciated. The surface of the picture appears to sparkle due to the vibrant optical effects produced by the interwoven colours.

Brian Gallagher
Still Life with Plums
34 x 42cm (13½ x 16½in)

HATCHING AND CROSSHATCHING

In hatching, an area of tone or colour is rendered by making a series of close, parallel strokes that appear to the eye as a solid area. The broken nature of hatching, when seen at a normal viewing distance, produces a more vibrant quality than flat areas of tone because the individual colours retain their identity.

Considerable variations of tone and texture can be achieved by varying the pressure on the pastel stick and the spaces between the strokes; the heavier and closer the strokes the more solid the tone will appear.

You can also lay one set of hatched lines over another, in opposite directions, to create complex colour effects. This technique is known as crosshatching. If you want to build up a really dense, textural effect, you can add still more strokes in yet another direction. Hatched lines can be thick or thin, curved, tapered or broken, crisp or ragged. You can use consistent strokes that follow the forms they are describing, or vary the angles and directions of the strokes to create a vigorous, energetic surface.

Finely hatched lines can be produced by breaking off a small piece of pastel and drawing with a broken edge. Alternatively, sharpen the end of the stick with a blade.

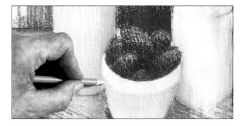

Pastel pencils are ideal for linear techniques such as hatching and crosshatching as they can be sharpened to a fine point or a chisel edge suitable for working on detailed areas.

STILL LIFE WITH PLUMS

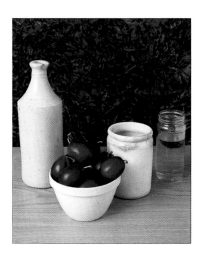

Left: The artist chose this small group of light-coloured containers for three reasons. First, they compose a natural harmony of repeated shapes and forms. Second, they create a dramatic effect when set against a dark background. And third, there are wonderful subtleties of tone and hue to be explored in the individual items and recreated using overlaid strokes of colour.

Materials and Equipment

- SHEET OF PALE GREY PASTEL PAPER • SOFT PASTELS: MID-TONE PERMANENT ROSE, LIGHT AND MID-TONES OF SAP GREEN, LIME GREEN, COBALT BLUE IN DARK, LIGHT AND VERY LIGHT TINTS, DARK ULTRAMARINE BLUE, DARK BLUE-VIOLET, LIGHT AND DARK TINTS OF VIOLET, PALE MAUVE, MID-TONE BLUE-GREY, TURQUOISE, LIGHT AND MID-TONES OF RAW SIENNA, MID-TONE BURNT SIENNA, LIGHT AND MID-TONES OF BURNT UMBER • HARD ERASER

1

Lightly draw the containers with a dark cobalt blue pastel. Sketching horizontal and vertical construction lines through the centres of the shapes will also help you draw the shapes accurately. Vary the weight of the lines, starting lightly at the top and and making stronger, more energetic lines where the forms meet the table. This "lost and found" quality suggests weight, solidity and light. Carry the lines down to suggest the reflections on the table, and blend the pigment into the paper to begin to suggest form.

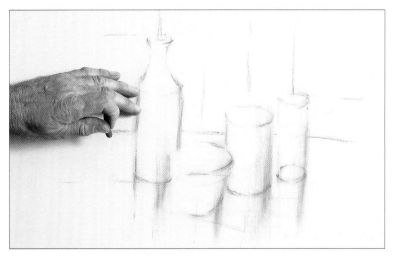

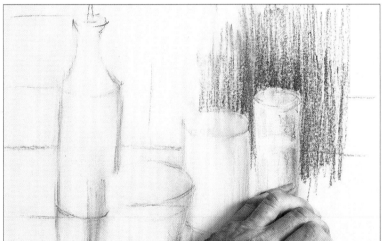

2

Block in the stone jar and the jam jar with vertical hatched strokes of light sap green overlaid with a mid-tone raw sienna, again dragging the colour down to suggest the reflections on the table. Soften some of the marks, but avoid over-blending. Start to fill in the background with vertical hatched strokes of dark cobalt blue overlaid with mid-tone permanent rose. Indicate the reflection of this colour in the jam jar, blending with your fingertip to lighten the tone.

3

Establish the horizontal plane of the table using mid-tone burnt sienna and burnt umber applied with loose, rapid hatching worked diagonally and vertically. Again, this colour is reflected in the jam jar. Apply more overlaid strokes of sap green and raw sienna to the stone jar, adding strokes of pale mauve for the cast shadow on the left. Develop the background tone with strokes of dark ultramarine blue.

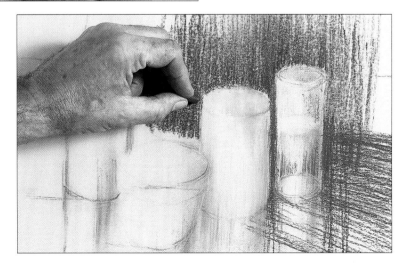

4

Draw the plums with dark ultramarine blue, then hatch with dark violet and permanent rose for the deep tones. Darken the background behind the bowl of plums with strokes of burnt umber and dark violet; this throws the plums forward and creates visual space. Develop the warm mid-tones on the plums with touches of burnt sienna, following the rounded contours with your pastel marks. Use a sharp corner of a hard eraser to clean up the drawing and to pull out some light tones, for example, those on the bowl.

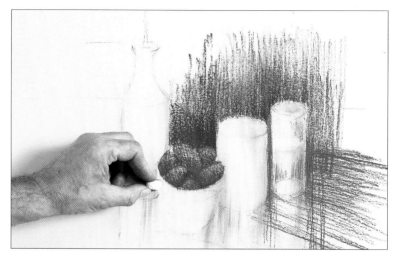

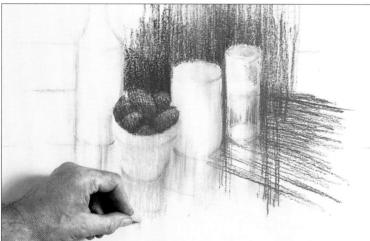

5

Work on the bowl using vertical hatching with turquoise and light cobalt blue. Define the shadow under the rim and base with light violet. Add some strokes of mid-tone sap green for the deeper tones and very light cobalt blue for the highlight on the left. Follow the pastel marks through into the reflection on the table so that the bowl becomes anchored to the table and does not appear "pasted on".

6

For the stone bottle and its reflection use light sap green overlaid with light raw sienna. Add lime green for the light areas and light burnt umber for the warm shadow tones. Continue blocking in the wooden table with diagonal hatching using mid-tone burnt sienna and burnt umber. Work over the rim of the bowl with very light cobalt blue to lighten the tone.

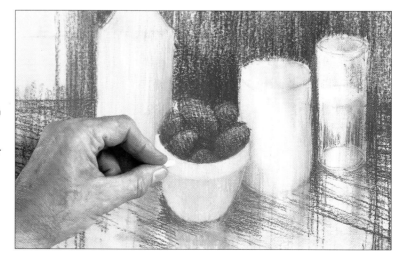

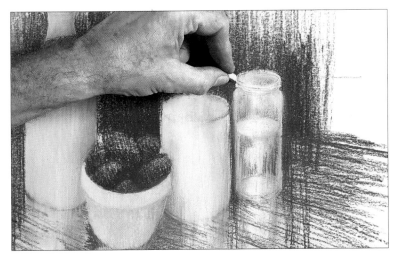

7

Define the highlights and reflections on the jar of water. Use mid-tone sap green in the water and on the shoulders of the jar. Show the reflection of the background at the back of the jar with blended tones of ultramarine blue and permanent rose. Define the ellipse of the water's surface with mid-tone blue-grey and the highlights on the rim of the jar with very light cobalt blue.

8

Define the rim of the stone jar and the highlights on the stone bottle with very light cobalt blue. Draw the two stray plums in the foreground with the same colours that were used for the plums in the bowl. Use some sap green and raw umber for the stalks. Complete the hatching on the table with burnt sienna and burnt umber warmed with hints of permanent rose.

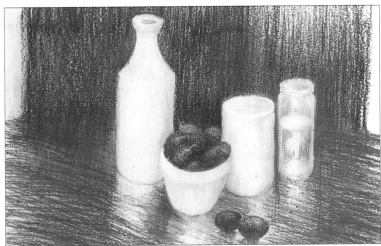

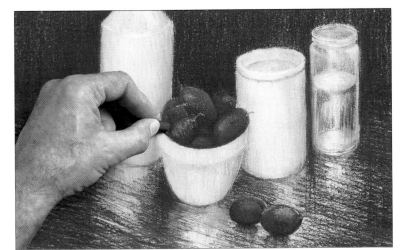

9

Continue working all over the image, refining the subtle nuances of colour. Build up the density of colour in the background with strokes of dark blue-violet and permanent rose. Put in the shadow beneath the rim of the stone jar with mid-tone blue-grey. Finally, build up the forms of the plums with further strokes of dark violet and permanent rose and use very pale raw sienna to put in the soft highlights.

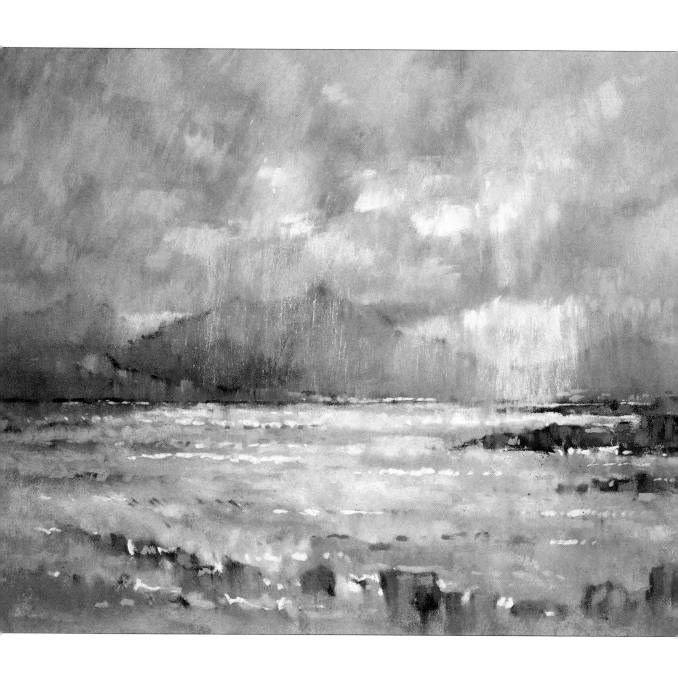

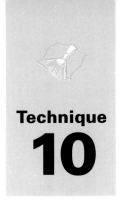

USING GLASSPAPER

S oft pastels can be used on any surface that is rough enough to provide a "key" that will retain the grains of colour. The support used for this painting is a type of fine glasspaper manufactured for smoothing wood, which also happens to be ideal for pastel painting.

The artist is interested in capturing the feel and atmosphere of space in his landscapes, and finds that working on glasspaper enables him to achieve subtle colour nuances descriptive of the transient effects of light and weather. The heavily toothed surface of this paper grips the particles of pastel pigment well and enables crisp mark-making, but also gives a slightly softened edge to the pastel strokes. As the colours are overlaid they soften and merge, giving a lush, painterly effect. At the same time, the grainy, crumbly texture of the pastel marks is retained, creating rich, dense qualities of colour and texture that add to the surface interest of the picture.

Geoff Marsters
Scottish Loch, Evening
38 x 49cm (15 x 19in)

PAINTING ON GLASSPAPER

Fine glasspaper – the kind used by carpenters for finishing and smoothing wood surfaces – makes an excellent support for painting with pastels. Its gritty, abrasive surface grips the particles of colour firmly, allowing you to overlay many colours and build up a rich, expressive surface. It also has a mellow buff tint which, when allowed to show through the overlaid strokes, enhances the bright pastel colours and provides a unifying middle tone.

Because glasspaper holds the pigment so firmly the finished picture requires little or no fixing. Its only disadvantage is that it does shave off the pastel fairly rapidly – and it is hard on the knuckles if you hold them too close to the paper!

Glasspaper (also known as flour paper) is available in various surface grains. Most artists choose the finest grade for pastel work – rough grades shave off too much pastel. It is available from art suppliers in large sheets, which you can then cut down to the size you want. Hardware stores stock small sheets (roughly A4 size) which are handy for sketching and small-scale work.

Sansfix paper, available from larger art suppliers, is similar to very fine glasspaper. Its surface is made from a thin layer of fine cork particles and grips the pastel particles so well that fixing is not necessary.

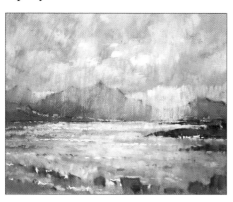

The gritty surface of glasspaper allows for both subtle blendings and crisp strokes with plenty of "bite".

SCOTTISH LOCH, EVENING

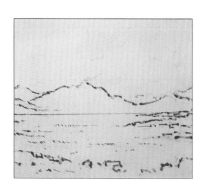

1

Plot the main structure of the composition with a dark purple pastel, placing the horizon line just below centre. Draw the outline of the mountains and indicate the rocks and water in the foreground with sketchy, broken lines.

Materials and Equipment

• SHEET OF FINE GRADE GLASSPAPER • SOFT PASTELS: PALE PINK, PALE CREAM, PALE YELLOW, GOLDEN YELLOW, PALE BLUE, COBALT BLUE, TURQUOISE BLUE, GREY-PURPLE, DARK PURPLE, MAUVE, PALE, DARK AND MID-TONE VIOLETS, PALE OCHRE AND OFF-WHITE • SOFT TISSUES

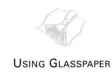

USING GLASSPAPER

2

Start to place a few strokes of local colour around the image to emphasize shapes and indicate tonal values. Here, the artist is applying cobalt blue and grey-purple over the mountains and the loch, using short lengths of pastel on their sides to stroke the colour on gently with short, vertical strokes.

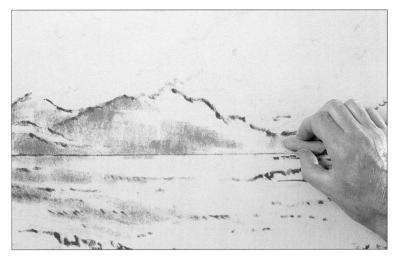

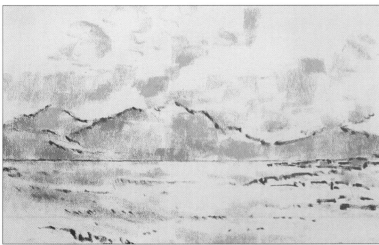

3

Continue building up the picture loosely, adding some touches of mauve and pale violet to the mountains and water. Start to draw in the main cloud formations with loose strokes and curls of pale violet, again using the long edge of the pastel stick and varying the pressure applied in order to describe the different "weights" of cloud.

4

Suggest the craggy forms of the rocks on the right of the picture and in the foreground with small strokes of dark violet and mid-tone violet. Use tiny broken pieces of pastel on their sides to build up blocks of colour and tone rather than drawing an outline and filling it in.

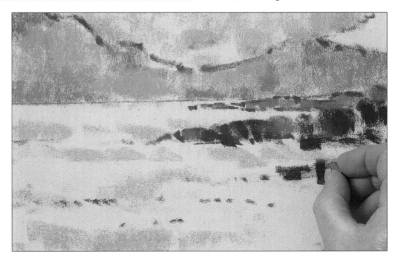

5

Don't work on any one area of the painting in isolation but continue adding touches of colour over the whole image. Loosely fill in the mountains with small side strokes, using a variety of warm and cool greys, blues, pinks and violets. Suggest the light ripples in the water with very pale pinks and blues, and echo the same colours in the sky.

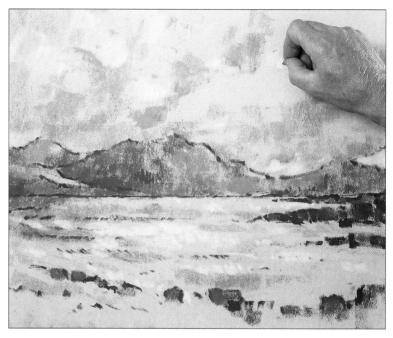

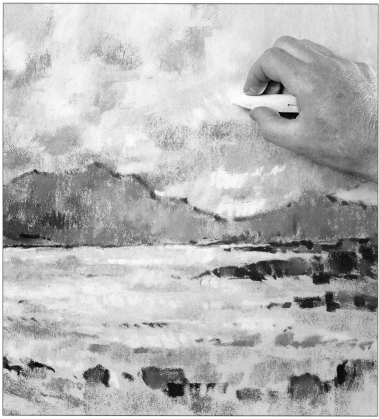

6

Scumble some warm cobalt blue into the foreground, to bring it forward in the picture plane. Now start to introduce some pale creams, ochres and yellows into the sky and the water with small marks and scribbles. Stroke the colours on lightly and let them meld with the colours already laid down.

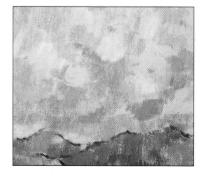

Above: This close-up detail of the sky reveals how the rough texture of the glasspaper breaks up the pastel marks, particularly where light pressure is applied, creating the effect of soft, vapourous clouds.

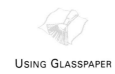

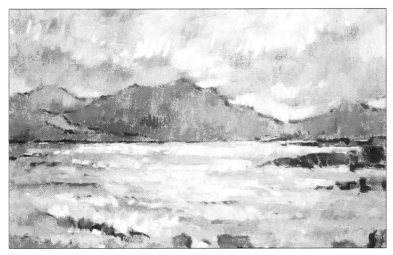

7

Develop subtle colour nuances in the sky with a combination of open-textured side strokes and lively scribbled marks. Vary the pressure on the pastels to produce different weights of colour that suggest three-dimensional form. Bring some of the sky colours down over outline of mountains to give the effect of evening mist. Once again, echo the sky colours in the water, using short dashes and upward flicks to convey sparkle and movement.

8

Now work across the sky using a tightly crumpled piece of tissue to partially blend the pastel marks. Apply very light pressure – just enough to soften the colours and describe the vapourous clouds, but without overblending. Use the same technique on the mountains, applying slightly more pressure to push more of the pastel pigment into the grain of the paper and deepen and intensify the colours.

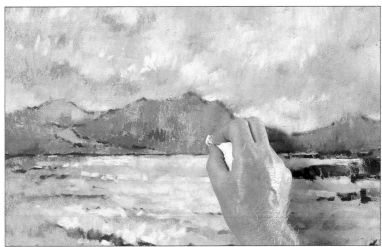

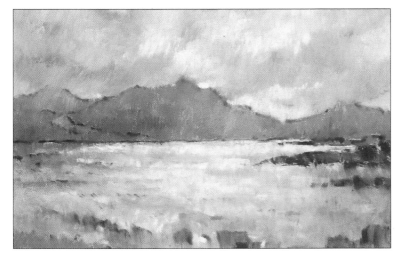

9

Continue softening the colours across the whole image, using clean pieces of tissue so as not to dirty the colours as you stroke over them. This process pushes more of the pastel pigment into the grain of the glasspaper, allowing you to apply further colours on top.

10

Put in a few touches of golden yellow and ochre in the sky near the horizon to indicate the setting sun peeping through the clouds. Use a warm off-white for the fluffy clouds that appear higher up. To create the effect of shafts of light striking through the clouds, snap off a short length of very pale soft yellow pastel and lightly skim it down through the sky and into the mountains with vertical strokes.

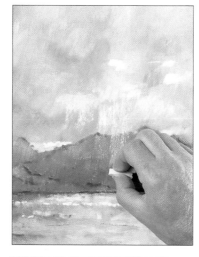

11

Continue stroking soft yellow over the mountains with a feather-light touch so that they appear veiled in mist. Work on the water with broken, horizontal lines of pale yellow and off-white to suggest light from the sky reflecting off the surface. These more linear, edgy marks provide a textural contrast to the veils of pastel colour and help to emphasize the impression of space.

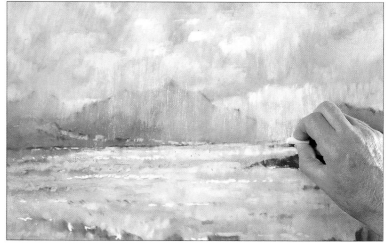

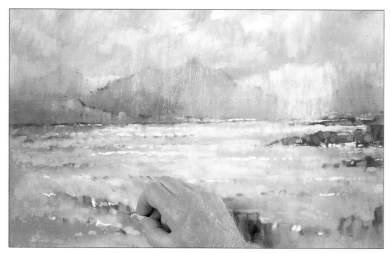

12

Finish off by adding some small, sharp hints of intense colour in the foreground using golden yellow on the rocks and turquoise blue on the water. Avoid fixing the finished picture as this will darken the colours; store it carefully until it can be framed behind glass.

SUPPLIERS

UNITED KINGDOM
Copystat Cardiff Ltd
44 Charles Street
Cardiff CF1 4EE
Tel: 01222 344422
Tel: 01222 566136 (mail order)
(general art suppliers)

Daler-Rowney Ltd
12 Percy Street
London W1A 9BP
Tel: 0171 636 8241
(painting and drawing materials)

John Mathieson & Co
48 Frederick Street
Edinburgh EH2 1HG
Tel: 0131 225 6798
(general art supplies)

L Cornelissen & Son Ltd
105 Great Russell Street
London WC1B 3LA
Tel: 0171 636 1045
(general art supplies)

Winsor & Newton
51 Rathbone Place
London W1P 1AB
Tel: 0171 636 4231
(painting and drawing materials)

SOUTH AFRICA
Art & Craft & Hobbies
72 Hibernia Street
P.O. Box 9635
George 6530
Tel: (0441) 74 1337
(Also offers all-hours nationwide
mail-order service)

Art Supplies
16 Ameshof Street
Braamfontein
Gauteng
Tel: (011) 339 2268

The Artist's Friend
Russel House, 41 Sir Lowry Road
Cape Town
Tel: (021) 45 4027 Fax: (021) 461 2901

Herbert Evans Art Shop
Cnr. Nugget and Jeppe Sts.
Johannesburg
Tel: (011) 402 2040

In-Fin-Art
9 Wolfe Street
Wynberg, Cape Town
Tel: (021) 761 2816 Fax: (021) 761 1884

PW Story
18 Foundry Lane
Durban
Tel: (031) 306 1224

Shop 148
The Pavilion
Westville
Tel: (031) 265 0250

AUSTRALIA
Art Stretchers Co Pty Ltd
188 Morphett Street
Adelaide South Australia 5000
Tel: (08) 212 2711

Artiscare
101 York Street
South Melbourne, Victoria 33205
Tel: (03) 9699 6188

Creative Hot Shop
96b Beaufort Street
Perth, Western Australia 6000
Tel: (08) 328 5437

Eckersley's
Cnr. Edward and Mary Streets
Brisbane, Queensland 4000
Tel: (07) 3221 4866

Oxford Art Supplies
221–223 Oxford Street
Darlinghurst NSW 2010
Tel: (02) 360 4066

NEW ZEALAND
Draw-Art Supplies Ltd
5 Mahunga Drive
Mangere
Tel: (09) 636 4862

The French Art Shop
51 Ponsonby Road
Ponsonby
Tel: (09) 379 4976

Gordon Harris
Art & Drawing Office Supplies
4 Gillies Avenue
Newmarket
Tel: (09) 520 4466

Studio Art Supplies (Parnell) Ltd
225 Parnell Road
Parnell
Tel: (09) 377 0302

Takapuna Art Supplies
18 Northcroft Street
Takapuna
Tel: (09) 489 7213

UNITED STATES
Art Supply Warehouse
360 Main Avenue
Norwalk
CT 06851
Tel: (800) 243 5038
(general art supplies – mail order)

Creative Materials Catalog
P.O. Box 1267
Gatesburg
IL 61401
Tel: (800) 447 8192
(general art supplies – mail order)

Hofcraft
P.O. Box 1791
Grand Rapids
MI 49501
Tel: (800) 435 7554
(general art supplies – mail order)

Pearl Paints
308 Canal Street
New York
NY 10013–2572
Tel: (800) 415 7327
(general art supplies – mail order)

INDEX

PICTURE CREDITS
The author and publishers would like to
thank the following for permission to repro-
duce additional photographs:

Visual Arts Library: pages 6–9

Index compiled by Susan Bosanko